More ...
Cobblestones
Cottages and
Castles

To Hilary

Happy Christmas
& Best wishes

David Dumn
& Kim

More ...
Cobblestones
Cottages and
Castles

DAVID YOUNG

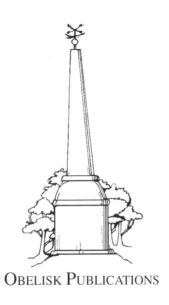

OBELISK PUBLICATIONS

*T*his book is dedicated to
the memory of
Kit Davies
close friend and director of "Cobblestones"

"All things will pass away,
Nothing remaining but death
And the Glory of Deeds"

Scandinavian Eddas

Published in association with TSW and Young Productions
Repro work by Equinox Scanning & Planning, Torquay, Devon

First published in 1992 by
Obelisk Publications
2 Church Hill, Pinhoe, Exeter, Devon EX4 9ER, England
Design and Layout by Chips and Sally Barber

© **David Young 1992**
ISBN: 0 946651 64 7

 Contents

                                                    Page

One
CURIOSITIES..9

Two
THATCH AND MATCH 23

Three
THE CHRIST CONNECTION 35

Four
FOLLIES..49

Five
BARS AND JARS 62

Six
GOD'S ACRE 76

Seven
MANOR HOUSES....................................87

∾ *Acknowledgements* ∾

My thanks to:
The National Trust
English Heritage
Exmoor National Park Authority
TSW Television South West
Christopher Woodard, for the benefit of his 30 years of research on
"The Christ Connection"
Dr Michael Ridley and Tim Batty for use of
the Tutenkhamen Exhibition photographs
Ken and Win Gribble for use of their drawing of "Ken at Midnight"
The Bigbury Mint
Terry Knight, master thatcher for use of himself
Cliff Vincent for use of various photographs
The television production team: Kit Davies, John Loveless, David Howarth, Trevor
Matthews, Steve Beech, Linda Buxton, Paul Roberts and Norman Erneshaw
My co-directors of Young Productions (South West) Ltd, Geoffrey Bullivant and
Margot Young
and to her for the many hours she worked to produce the typescript
Sally and Chips Barber, thoughtful and considerate publishers
And all those lovely people who so kindly let me into their homes and establishments.

Plate Acknowledgements

All sketches, plans and majority of photographs by the author.
Thanks to Chips Barber for photographs on pages:
18, 19, 20, 26, 27, 31, 51, 58, 75 and 76. Also for
Front Cover showing cottages at Branscombe in East Devon
Back Cover by Guy of Chagford

*F*oreword

by Rt Hon Paddy Ashdown MP

HOUSE OF COMMONS
LONDON SW1A 0AA

15 August 1992

   In these days, when there is, properly, a lot of talk about preserving our natural environment, it is too easy to forget that our "environment" is not natural at all, but man made.

   Our towns, our villages, the very shape of our countryside bear the personal mark of our forbears who made this countryside what it is. And the stamp of these people is in the very stones of the buildings and the shape of the fields.

   For me it is the human dimension which makes this most beautiful part of Britain so fascinating.

   I suppose almost no-one has brought the human dimension of the South West more alive for more people, than David Young.

   In the first "Cobblestones" and perhaps even more through his television programmes, he has combined a sharp, architect's eye with a deep love of the area and knowledge of its history, to uncover a South West which even those of us privileged enough to live here did not know existed.

   And yet this is not a book just about architectural detail and historical knowledge. Here you will also find humour and those little intimate insights which make the past live and the present more interesting.

   If you know David Young's work you will know what to expect and you will not be disappointed, for this is David at his very best. If, by any chance, you haven't yet come across David Young's work before, then you have a treat in store for you.

   Enjoy it! I did!

❦ *One* ❧
CURIOSITIES

Lydford
DEVON

Loomed over by Dartmoor, Lydford with its spectacular gorge, Norman church and Norman castle has just about everything to offer. And so it should, for at one time, after Exeter, it was the most important town in Devon, which served as a centre for the smelting of silver as well as tin and was also in Saxon times a Royal mint.

The coins minted back in those days were called Lydford pennies: silver pennies which are something like a thousand years old. The collection on display in the Castle Inn contains slightly more than exist in the British Museum. The king responsible for

minting the coins was Ethelred the Unready. I never could understand why he was 'unready'; probably because he was unprepared for his wedding night, for his first son Edward the Confessor did not turn up until five or six years later.

The silver penny was a hammered penny, a flat disc of silver imprinted on one side, turned over with a die, and hammered on the other side. That silver penny's value then was something in the region of forty pounds, quite a lot of money. In fact on the back it has a little cross, and dividing it up you got four farthings, so a quarter of that coin was worth about ten pounds in those days.

The pub itself, the Castle Inn, was originally an old house, and the lintel over the fireplace is Norman, but it was not actually built as a Norman fireplace because, like much of the stone used to build the house it was pinched from the castle next door.

All that remains today of the great Norman castle is the keep, built in 1195 at a cost of £84. Comparative costs between then and now put that figure in the region of half a million pounds, and don't forget building labour was cheap in those days – literally slave labour. It was built as a prison for stannary law offenders – tinners had the privilege of being tried by their own kind. Well, some privilege that turned out to be, because they fell under Lydford Law which was absolutely unique. It was summed up by a local poet, a chap named Brown, and the first verse of his poem read:

"I oft have heard of Lydford Law
How in the morn they hang and draw
And sit in judgement after."

And really that is exactly what happened, because they hanged, drew and quartered them in the morning and had the trial in the afternoon. I only hope they found them guilty. To me this is an evil place, horror seems to emanate from the very walls. And I'm not the only one to feel this, for you rarely see a bird inside the gaunt walls, the point being that birds dislike places of horror.

The walls are ten feet thick, and only one man is known to have escaped from here. His name was Richard Strode and he was M.P. for Plympton. He had fallen foul of the stannary laws and had been locked up inside. He bribed his way out and went hot foot to Parliament. That was Henry

VIII's parliament in London, and there he raised the law of parliamentary privilege, whereby you could make a statement about anybody or anything within the precincts of the House and not be sued or sent back to a prison like this. That privilege still exists today.

The castle is beautifully looked after by English Heritage and there are galleries from which we can see the place perfectly.

They are reminiscent to me of the galleries in the great prison which took over from here at Princetown. Next to the Tower of London this is the oldest prison in Britain.

Immediately adjacent and well within screaming distance of the prison is St Petroc's Church. I find its proximity to such a place of horror surprising even today. Perhaps it was placed here to be on hand to gather up the departing souls of the cruelly executed prisoners.

Probably the oldest thing in the church is a tub font, thought to be dating from Norman times, but I personally think it's even earlier. It could be Saxon, and if that is the case then it's as old as the Lydford penny.

What is fascinating about the font is all that is left of the original cover is a hinge. For in the year 1236 the then Archbishop of Canterbury decreed that all fonts should actually have lockable covers, simply because people were pinching the holy water and using it for all sorts of nefarious purposes, including witchcraft.

In my travels around the South West I keep coming across the Pinwill sisters. These were ladies who, back in Victorian times, were actually wood carvers. And the screen here was carved by Violet Pinwill and is probably one of the most charming bits of her work ever seen, for it's a complete copy of a medieval rood screen.

Something quite exciting which is a rare find is the pew given by Edward VIII, that is the king who abdicated when he was Duke of Cornwall. I love it really because the bench end is quite superb: it has a figure of Edward the Confessor, and he is holding a model of Westminster Abbey.

Bigbury Mint
DEVON

The Bigbury Mint at Ermington in Devon is the last of its kind in the country, if not in the world. Minting is a simple process: they hammer a die on to a flat piece of metal and make an impression, then, turning it over, do the same thing on the other side. Coins minted here in the late eighteenth and early nineteenth centuries were made from copper. Mined in the Tavistock area, these coins, or as they were colloquially known 'chips', could be used in the mine shops. In fact today there is still a hamlet in the Tavistock area called 'Chip Shop'. Coins like the Lydford penny would have been made in this way.

They are quite simply a token. A hammered coin is very thin, just about as thin as it is possible to hammer out a piece of silver.

Despite the primitive way in which early coins were hand struck, their appearance was entirely due to the skill of the engraver. It is often said that with mass production today, real craftsmanship is dead. What nonsense! For although coins are mass produced, thanks to modern materials and sophisticated methods, their appearance is entirely reliant on the engravers who pour their unique skill into the design and production of the original die. A skill, handed down through the centuries, requiring the delicate touch of the surgeon, enormous wrist strength, and above all a creative mind.

The first coins ever were minted about 700 BC in Lydia, which is now part of Turkey. Money in those days simply consisted of lumps of gold or silver until somebody hit on the idea of marking these pieces of metal. Up until that time, before embarking on a business transaction, the metal had to be assayed in order to prove that it was either gold or silver. Once these marks of value had started to appear, you could be confident that they were recognisable

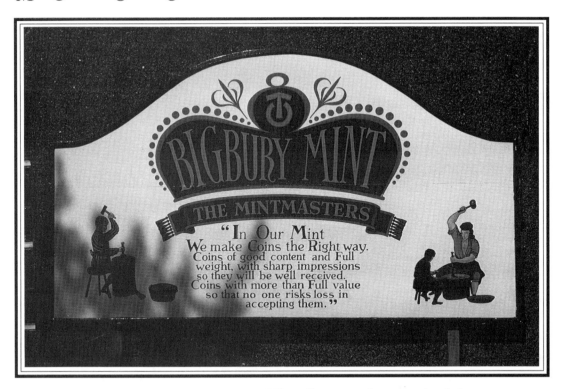

as to the silver and gold content. It was King Croesus who organised the system on a national basis, and he started the minted coin as we know it today.

Strangely enough, the gold hand-minted coin is still in demand today. The Bigbury Mint has recently been commissioned for a new venture, and has been involved with a gold mine in Fiji, minting legal tender coins for the Fijian government. Because hand minting means that they have irregular edges, rather like the old Greek and Roman coins,

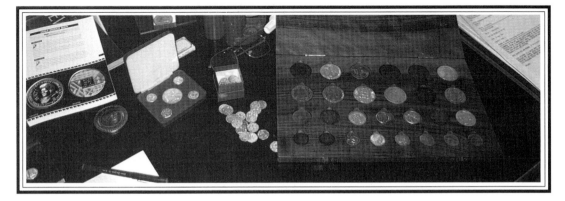

this system of minting fitted the Fijian requirements perfectly, and the Bigbury Mint was invited to design and strike the new coins. The final result is a set of lovely 18 carat gold coins, a credit to the South West of England craftsmanship.

Tutankhamen Exhibition
DORCHESTER, DORSET

Gold. For thousands of years now, the golden rule seems to have been that he who holds the gold rules the day, and this was certainly the case when the boy King Tutankhamen was in charge of Egypt. Despite the realistic appearances of the display

at the Tutankhamen Exhibition in Dorchester, we are not in Egypt but the heart of Dorset. There is today a breath of fresh air blowing through our museums. No longer are they dull Victorian buildings packed with dusty glass cases full of musty pieces of Roman pottery, but exhibitions alive with activity and music. And so it is with the reconstruction of the finding of the young Pharaoh's tomb, designed and built by Dr Michael Ridley.

It was on the 25th of November 1922 that Howard Carter and Lord Carnarvon made, what was at the time, the greatest of archeological finds. The Exhibition's royal burial chamber is reproduced and looks almost exactly as it did when completed 3,300 years ago.

There are old photographs of course, and they help set up the story, but there are also surprises. Face to face with the young Pharaoh for the first time can be an unnerving experience!

This exhibition is considered to be one of the finest of its kind anywhere, so much so that Michael Ridley has been asked to reproduce his reconstruction in Egypt. An accolade if ever there was one!

I think had I been there at the time I would have been as overawed as the group of figures in the ante-chamber. To capture the atmosphere at that moment seems to be nigh on impossible, but here they have succeeded beyond belief. But that is the whole idea of the exhibition – to make you feel as if you are actually there.

Howard Carter made a small hole in the wall of the ante-chamber and was overwhelmed by what he saw. I too could not resist a quick peep. The room was packed full of goodies. What an experience. In this display you can actually see through the aperture and feel that you too are there.

Predominant are wonderful animal-shaped funereal beds on which Tutenkhamen's three coffins were brought to the tomb. Underneath are sacks of grain – food parcels supplied to provide sustenance on resurrection day.

In the burial chamber itself, scaffolding was needed to help raise the heavy coffins, for one of them was solid gold. There was much talk at the time of an ancient curse on anyone who opened the tomb, Lord Carnarvon died just five months later, of a mosquito bite. At that moment all the lights in Cairo went out, and back on his estate in England his dog howled, just once, and he too died. Coincidence perhaps, who knows?

Dr Michael Ridley has provided us with a superb replica of one of history's major events, and one well worth a visit.

Ken Gribble's Screen
SIDMOUTH, DEVON

Great discoveries are not always found below ground, sometimes they are staring you in the face. When artist Ken Gribble bought his home in Sidmouth, he not only bought himself a house but a national treasure as well: a unique painted timber wall, dating from Tudor times, in a poor state of repair. Painstakingly, using his immense talents, he set about restoring it. Months passed by before he realised that unseen hands were guiding his.

One night during the winter of 1966, with the wind howling down Chapel Street, raging in from the West, then it is all too easy to imagine happenings from the past. Ken was working very late with labrador Jasper his only companion. when he suddenly felt very conscious that he had strayed on to a strange wave length, repeating something that some one else had done before. Ken looked at Jasper, the dog looked at him, he turned the lights out and both scooted off to bed!

Ken was unaware before he was 'taken over' just how exciting a find this was, although it was always understood to have been a work of importance. It was thought to have been the work of monks who had done a certain amount of finger painting, perhaps on a wet Sunday afternoon. In the heraldry portrayed on the screen you can read the history of England for the three hundred years before the times of Elizabeth. Half of the arms are of France and half of England. The supporters are the golden lions, strong heraldic supporters, and the strongest of all – the dragon – seen sometimes as the serpent. Above is the Tudor crown which was lost by Charles II, again surrounded by a lion and there is Elizabeth Domini Regina as abbreviations. Above this is a coat of arms and the motto "*Honi soit qui mal y pense*".

The whole chapter of events in Sidmouth, or Sid as it was, relates to the fact that it belonged to the church from 1066 right through the centuries until 1639. The property was owned in turn by Henry VIII, Edward the boy King, Mary, that is Bloody Mary, and Elizabeth who held it until she died in 1603, when it was inherited by James I.

How fortunate for future generations that this unique treasure should have fallen into such capable and caring hands as those of artist Ken Gribble.

The Palm House
BICTON, DEVON

The impressive Palm House in Bicton Park in East Devon is like a miniature version of the Crystal Palace. It is a great bubble of glass which predates William Paxton's famous exhibition hall by a good 25 years, and may well have been the source of Paxton's inspiration.

It was built in 1825 by Lord George Rolle as a giant greenhouse for his wife to house exotic plants and fruit. The aim to create rain-forest conditions was entirely successful, humidity being supplied by a misting unit high up in the roof, delivering atomised water that disperses as it falls.

There is no forced rhubarb in this particular greenhouse, but a glorious collection of delights such as bananas and pineapples. Pineapples were a delicacy in those days, often hired out as a feature at dinner tables for one guinea, plus another guinea if eaten! Begonias cover the ground with colour, and as a complement to the heavy fragrance there is the delightful sound of water falling into the pool which houses aquatic plants and carp.

The central dome is self-supporting with no strengthening rafters or principal ribs whatever.

Bicton Gardens

Amazingly it is held together by pressure alone, and only became stable when glazed. There are at least 18,000 scalloped pieces of glass, overlapping like fish scales. Each original pane was hand-moulded to be thicker at the edges and thinner in the middle, cleverly allowing water to run down the centre away from the wrought iron ribs.

In 1985 huge scale refurbishment was found to be necessary, and after months of expert work, which included the complete re-bedding of each pane of glass, this glorious building now stands firm – a testament to craftsmen and craftsmanship from two vastly different centuries.

Pinwill Sisters
ERMINGTON, DEVON

Ermington Church in South Devon with its crooked spire is one of our luckier churches for very often Victorian restorers, in spite of their good intentions, managed to destroy more than they preserved. So much so that many examples of medieval craftsmanship were ripped out and lost for ever. Their excuse being that most of the timber screens and pews were so riddled with worm and death watch beetle that they had to be destroyed. However well meaning their intentions, they managed to strip many of our churches of the work of true medieval craftsmanship. In 1880 the interior was packed full of box pews, that's pews with their own separate doors, a gallery and an unusual Jacobean screen dating from the 1600s.

The gallery and the box pews have disappeared but the screen is still with us and the whole church is packed with the most beautiful woodwork I think I have ever seen. And therein lies one of the most amazing stories to have emerged from the Victorian era: for they were all carved by a young girl. Her name was Violet Pinwill and her father was rector here for many years. All of the woodwork was carved in the stable block of the rectory.

There were seven daughters altogether in the family, and Violet's mother decided that they should have a profession – an unusual idea in those days. She chose one which for girls at any rate was unusual as well as unique, the art of wood carving.

When restoration work started on the church, the girls were still in the schoolroom. Violet and two other sisters, Mary and Ethel, were taught the craft by craftsmen engaged on the task of the restoration work.

This massive pulpit was one of the first pieces that Violet tackled. It is solid oak and Violet was just 17 when she did the work. The carved figures on display include the figure of Christ, worked from one piece of material as is the scene with Peter receiving the keys. You can see the original thickness of the carved wood was something like six inches. It really is the most beautiful piece of work.

The girls worked in the traditions of the medieval craftsmen, and there isn't a better example of this than the font cover. It is beautifully fretworked and looks like a piece of fine lace. Such things cost money even in those days and they were paid for by members of the family, who stumped up enough money to get this sort of work done, on behalf of a deceased relative as a memorial.

The church is full of other much older treasures which have been skillfully restored.

There is an Elizabethan canopied tomb, rich in colour. Some of it is more recent colour and at high level you can see the original colouring which is much paler; this was applied back in 1580. It also serves as an altar, and you can see that even altars were not sacrosanct in those days because someone's carved the date 1704, perhaps it was some itinerant choirboy!

Another great treasure is a long slender banner, the funereal banner of a knight, which was hung in the church when he died. It is seventeenth century and fixed just below it are two helmets: one is his battle helmet and the other, with the spike on, is the funereal helm. This is also distinguishable because it has a very small aperture for the neck, too small in fact for him to get his neck through. This was placed on the top of his coffin during the committal ceremony.

Violet's finest work is the reredos behind the altar. The whole of the surround is cut from oak

and is full of evangelists and illustrations of various bible stories. Right in the centre is the crucifixion. It is however a clever piece of work for the focus of the reredos is the nativity, carved in alabaster. Like the woodwork, the carving is in great depth and most attractive.

Admiring this, it is not difficult to recall the words of the greatest story of all time which inspired this delicate work of art:

"And so Joseph went up to Bethlehem and with him went Mary who was betrothed to him. She was expecting a child and while they were there, the time came for her baby to be born and she gave birth to a son, her first born, she wrapped him in swaddling clothes and laid him in a manger because there was no room at the Inn."

——— ❧ *Two* ☙ ———
THATCH AND MATCH

The Royal Oak
WINSFORD, SOMERSET

The Royal Oak at Winsford in West Somerset lies on the old pack-horse route across Exmoor, and the narrow pack-horse bridge is still here. Irish yarn landed at Minehead was traded for mineral ore taken from the moor.

This superb fourteenth century inn with its cascading thatched roof is internationally famous, for it features on British travel posters throughout the world as the finest example of a perfect English inn.

The thatched roof is a superb example of the thatcher's art, with beautifully constructed animals. Even the entrance porch has a delightful thatched roof.

The fireplace in the main bar complete with cauldron and kettle does not look as though it has changed since the inn was the haunt of the highwayman Tom Faggis, who was immortalised in the novel "*Lorna Doone*".

I was greeted with true Exmoor hospitality by proprietor and landlord Charlie Steven. The inn is a venue for shooting parties during the season, and its proximity to the Exmoor stag hunt is recorded on a huge mural which fills the walls of the lounge.

The Royal Forest of Exmoor was never wooded – it was the hunting ground of Kings. From medieval times the word "Forest" actually meant "Open hunting ground". It is said today there are still as many deer on Exmoor as there were in Queen Elizabeth I's reign.

I was not surprised to discover that the inn was reproduced years ago at the British Exhibition in New York as the typical English pub.

Abbotsbury
DORSET

Abbotsbury's once great abbey buildings have long since disappeared. All that is left is a rather forlorn looking archway. So where are the buildings? What has happened to them? They line the streets of Abbotsbury, one of Dorset's many lovely villages.

What happened was this: local people, wanting to build their own houses, went to the old Abbey buildings, pinched the stone – using it as a sort of quarry – then came back and put up their own homes. They did not just take the stones, they took the doors and windows as well, and you can not blame them really – it was there for the taking and this is what helps make this such a lovely village, the continuity of the colour of the stone.

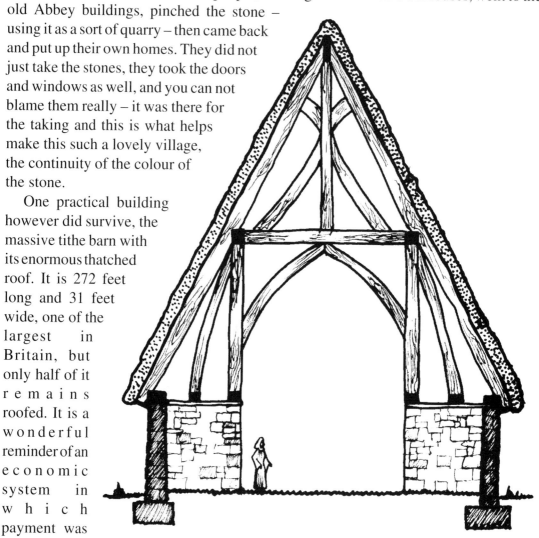

One practical building however did survive, the massive tithe barn with its enormous thatched roof. It is 272 feet long and 31 feet wide, one of the largest in Britain, but only half of it remains roofed. It is a wonderful reminder of an economic system in which payment was made in kind rather than in cash, which is why of course such barns were known as Tithe Barns.

A tithe was a tenth part of the annual profits from the occupation of land, it was levied in this country from the ninth century, as an ecclesiastical tax intended basically to support the monasteries and the parish priest.

Once harvested of course, the grain required processing. This was in two parts – threshing and winnowing. Threshing separated the ears of corn from the straw, whilst winnowing separated the grains from the chaff. So the great barns were both working places and store houses. One could say that they were our very first factories.

It is no coincidence that such barns are similar in design and structure to that of the

cathedrals and the larger churches – they were put up by the same builders.

Old Mother Hubbard
YEALMPTON, DEVON

There cannot be another village in England which, during the nineteenth century, had its history recorded in the form of a poem, the first verse of which is known by just about every adult and child in the country. It is the nursery rhyme "Old Mother Hubbard" which was written in the Devon village of Yealmpton. I am sure you will be as surprised as I was to discover that there are as many as 28 verses altogether which are no more really than a list of all the shops and pubs which existed in this tiny village when the nursery rhyme was composed in 1805.

It was written here at Kitley House by Sarah Martin on a visit to her sister, who was married to Squire Bastard, whose descendants still own the fine house. The rhyme is supposedly based on an old lady who was housekeeper at Kitley at that time. Sarah, incidentally, fell in love with a young naval lieutenant, but sadly marriage was not forthcoming, for he was the future King George IV who, despite returning Sarah's love, was obliged to marry elsewhere whilst Sarah remained a spinster.

It is generally understood that Old Mother Hubbard eventually retired to the charming 'fairy tale' cottage here at the Eastern end of the village. Just look at the shape of the walls and the undulations of its thatched roof. Is it not perfect? And can you imagine a better place for Old Mother Hubbard to have lived in?

One of the best known verses in the poem recounts how "the cupboard was bare" and that "the poor little doggy got none". And it is at this point that the rhyme becomes a social document as well as a record of village shops, for the bare cupboard is thought to refer to the severe shortage of food at that time, brought about by the Napoleonic Wars.

It was very much a farming village then, and was virtually self-contained with all the shops and services that the community required. It needed to be of course for, communications being what they were, a trip to Plymouth, seven miles away, was a major expedition.

Many of the shops referred to in the verses have now gone. No longer is there a hatter or a tailor, but the baker is still here, and as the appropriate verse tells us: "She went to the baker to get some bread, and when she came back the dog was dead". But don't worry, he must have been just faint with hunger for "She went to the tavern for white wine and red and when she came back the dog stood on his head". Perhaps he had had a swig or two of the wine?

Today new houses integrate into the village in a much more satisfactory way than new houses do in many other West Country villages, probably because of the use of traditional colourwash and rendering.

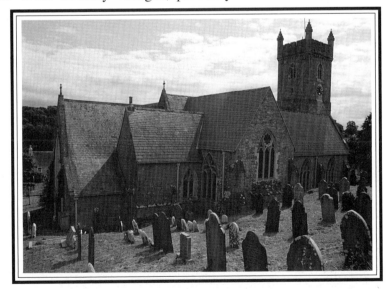

The main body of the parish church was rebuilt during Victorian times, but the tower was found to be unsafe and demolished in 1911. Money was not easily forthcoming, so "Old Mother Hubbard" came to the rescue, in the shape of the vicar, who wrote to village children under the pen name of "Old Mother Hubbard". It was taken up by the national press and brought in thousands of subscriptions from all over the world and the tower was rebuilt; a happy ending for all concerned. Poet Laureate, Sir John Betjeman, who delighted in Victorian and Edwardian architecture, described it as "The most amazing" Victorian church in Devon. The rhyme ends on a happy note as well, for the dog successfully "married", and as the last verse tells us: "The bride made a curtsy, the dog made a bow, the dame wished them joy and they both said bow-wow".

Thatched Brewery
BRIDPORT

Trust me to find the only thatched brewery in the country. There is no doubt about it either: no other premises would use a beer barrel instead of a pinnacle at the apex of the

roof as they do here. Situated in Bridport, Dorset, Palmer's Brewery is one of the oldest in the country and still very much a family concern.

Mind you, they are not that old fashioned down here in Dorset, the Victorian horse-drawn dray only makes the occasional appearance at very special events.

I don't know about you, but there is something about that form of transport. You can forget your modern two-litre vehicles, I will settle every time for one horse power!

Dalwood
DEVON

Probably the most delightful thatch building in the South West is the Loughwood Meeting House at Dalwood, near Axminster in East Devon. One of the earliest Baptist chapels in the country, it is now maintained by the National Trust. Amongst its main structural features is the unusual curved buttresses which help prop it up, for it is built on a hillside.

The reason for its isolated position is simply because in 1653 the Baptist congregation from nearby Kilmington sought refuge from persecution, Baptist Meeting houses being illegal at that time. The visiting preacher, obliged to come on horseback, stabled his horse here. A most suitable temporary kennel for Oliver whilst I took a look around the chapel.

Secrecy was such that the earliest meeting places were barns or cottages, and it is thought that the chapel may have been converted from a cottage. I have my doubts, for the ceiling is far too high. It may well, however,

have been built to look like cottages from the outside, to fool snoopers. It remains today virtually intact – austere but cheerful with its white walls, clear glass windows and unvarnished woodwork.

It is hard to realise that, despite being Christians and sharing the Bible with their persecutors, it did not stop the Baptists being ridiculed, imprisoned, transported, even killed. During baptisms, for example, they actually had guards outside to warn of the approach of soldiers, set upon enforcing the law.

The baptismal pool is quite deep with three stone steps leading down into it; water was obtained from a nearby spring.

The Reverend Isaac Hann, a celebrated pastor, was so highly thought of that he was actually buried in the chapel – a common practice in the Church of England which was frowned on by non-conformists. His memorial stone on the wall makes fascinating reading. He died in his 88th year, and the last verse on the memorial provides us with the following advice: "Reader think not to live so long, but seek to live as well."

Beneath the gallery are two rooms with fireplaces. Their presence illustrates the distance which the Baptists had to travel in order to worship. Whole Sundays were spent here requiring simple catering facilities.

The seating arrangements are simple box pews, a sort of home from home with tiny front doors, the idea being to keep out the draughts. The gallery was once used by players of stringed instruments, for there were church orchestras or bands before they were replaced by organs.

Broadhembury
DEVON

There is little doubt that the lovely village of Broadhembury in Devon owes much of its charm to delightful terraced cottages roofed with continuous thatch. On and on they go, undulating unceasingly over the cob walls, broken only by the occasional dormer window or gentle gabled end.

Devon boasts of so many thatched roofs for practical rather than aesthetic reasons. Most cottage walls were built of cob – a mixture of earth and small stones with the occasional strand or two of straw. I suppose you could call it poor man's concrete! Such walls, whilst waterproof, were not strong enough to take heavy roofing materials like clay tiles. Thatch, being lighter, was the answer.

There is something romantic about thatched roofs. Like pets, they cry out for attention, and in return they offer comfort and pleasure. Whilst being quite entranced by the curve of a nicely rounded gable, I find a modern angular concrete tiled roof a complete turn off. No wonder poets dreamt of ending their days in a thatched cottage!

Reminiscences of a Master Thatcher
SOMERSET

A master thatcher now since 1962, Terry Knight first spent a couple of years on a farm, where he learned the skills of hedging, spar making, reed cutting and thrashing. His interest turned to thatching and after five years of apprenticeship (it is only two years

now, incidentally) he became qualified in what is an art as well as a skill. Terry has vivid memories of his days as an apprentice: he was quite proud when his old boss left him on his own for the first time putting down the reed. Thinking he was doing a splendid job, he completed several yards packed "nice and tight" and left almost in the dark, thinking he had done a good job and was quite proud of himself. Next morning the boss said "What were you up to last night?" "What do you mean?" says Terry. "Well," came the reply, "there's a chimney up there somewhere. If you stand underneath, you can't see it any more!" True enough, enthusiasm and the approaching dusk had beaten him: the chimney was practically thatched as well! Terry went up and tried to pat it back, but the boss made him rip the lot off. He nearly cried, he was off the roof for about a fortnight and he had to keep fetching and carrying again! He never slipped up again.

It is hard to say what makes a good thatcher because no two thatchers work exactly the same way. Terry's apprentice has got his own style and he is already a good thatcher but they no longer work entirely together because his style of thatching is quite different to Terry's, although he is Terry's apprentice. If the boy works on the other side of the roof and Terry stays on his side then it is perfectly all right, but to work jointly would not be a success.

Terry uses French reed now because straw has such a short life, lasting in some cases only twelve years. Water reed is quicker and cleaner to use and he can phone his French suppliers and it is delivered within four days. That water reed lasts for 50 or 60 years whilst straw only lasts twelve years because it is too short and the comber cannot get out all the grain, and it often starts growing on the roof: water reed is also that much tougher. Straw wears at the rate of a quarter of an inch a year. Years ago red standard straw was used, this was five or six feet long and was specially grown for thatching. This does not seem to be the case any more.

Being a man of Somerset, Terry reckons that a good thatcher depends on a few pints of good cider at lunchtime. But only a few though – one pint too many and all the stuff looks twice the length and takes twice as long to put on! That is really one of Terry's jokes, for clambering about a roof requires immense concentration. It is too easy to twist around quickly and fall off the ladder.

He has only fallen off once in his life time and that was during his apprenticeship. He put down the locking bar which stops the ladder falling off the roof, thinking it would be all right. He climbed the ladder but it did not hold and down he went, ladder and all. It was a church roof and he finished up in a freshly dug grave! He reckons that "That one step to the grave could have been the quickest on record!" He still "dines out on the story".

Terry recalls an old saying among thatchers:

*"The job's done
The money's due
You're behind
And where be you?"*

If they don't pay up, "I can always take it all off again," he says, something which did once happen. The owner refused to pay, so he came back and took it all off! He ended up in court on a trespassing charge but he says, "I got away with it on the grounds that I'd only left my tools up there and had gone to fetch them." As a result no other thatcher in the area would carry out the work, and it was many

years before that thatch was replaced.

It is obvious that a sense of humour is important in what Terry admits is "a lonely old life up there", but he wouldn't change it for the world.

You do not have to be a painter or poet to create items of great beauty. Masters of their craft like Terry Knight are artists too. Perhaps we should equate the thatcher with the sculptor – both skillfully shaping thing of lasting beauty for our enjoyment – long may they continue to thrive.

⎯⎯ ∾ *Three* ∾ ⎯⎯
THE CHRIST CONNECTION

The Tradition

Legends and traditions generally spring from a basis of truth, and one of the strangest of these nurtured today in the South West of England is that Christ came here, not once but several times, first as a boy with his uncle, Joseph of Arimathea, and later as an adult, residing for some time at Glastonbury prior to the start of His ministry, at the age of 30, in the Holy Land.

This is surely enough in itself to explain the reverence afforded to Glastonbury over the centuries. But there is more: the Virgin Mary, Christ's mother is said to be buried somewhere in the crypt of St Joseph's chapel. Hence the meaning of the enigmatic carving on the South side of the main wall of the chapel 'JESUS-MARIA'.

Whilst there is no positive proof of Christ's visit to Britain, the aim is to show what evidence there is allowing you to form your own opinion. During the last fifteen years new facts have come to light, so today's historian has had to change his attitude.

The tradition, or legend, is made up of several separate and independent traditions which apparently, on the face of it, have no connection with each other. They fit together and present us with a consecutive story of the visit.

The first is found in Cornwall, and is recorded in the Rev. Baring-Gould's '*Book of Cornwall*' where he writes: "Another Cornish story is to the effect that Joseph of Arimathea came in a boat to Cornwall, and brought the boy Jesus with him, and then later taught him how to extract tin and purge it from its wolfram." Until recently when the tin was flashed, the tinner would shout "Joseph was in the tin trade!"

Another is found in Somerset concerning the coming of Christ and Joseph in a ship of Tarshish, and how they came to the Summer Land – as Somerset was then known – and journeying to a place called Paradise.

The next tradition is to be found in the village of Priddy, on the top of the Mendip Hills, to the effect that Our Lord and Joseph of Arimathea stayed there.

Finally, traditions associate Jesus Christ directly with Glastonbury. Joseph of Arimathea was one of the wealthiest merchants of his day. He actually held the position of Minister of Mines to the Roman Empire, and his fleet of ships were used to transport tin from Cornwall to all parts of the Empire. He was the Virgin Mary's uncle and after the death of Jesus' father he would have assumed responsibility for the boy. It seems logical that he should take the young Christ with him for there is no trace of his whereabouts in the Bible between the ages of seven and twelve. It was at the age of twelve that he features briefly in the Gospels at the Feast of the Passover when he visits the Temple.

Again, between the ages of twelve and thirty there is no mention of his whereabouts in the Bible. Legend and certain facts, gleaned from small amounts of written evidence passed down through the centuries, declare that he spent several of those years in quiet contemplation at Glastonbury. There he built for himself a small house of wattle and daub – in other words a sophisticated mud hut, similar in design and contemporary with the Glastonbury and Mere lake villages.

It was later, after Christ's crucifixion, that Joseph of Arimathea was forced to flee Palestine, arriving at Glastonbury with eleven companions, or disciples. Among them was Christ's mother, the Virgin Mary. But why come here, why not stay in France with

St Philip, one of the original disciples? The answer surely is simply, because it was where Jesus Christ had been, and where, in A. H. Lewis's view in '*Christ in Cornwall*', his mother spent the rest of her life. Here he says she died in about AD 48, and here she lies buried.

It certainly bears consideration. Why, for example, is England called 'Our Lady's Dowry'? The Roman Catholic Church knows of the title. Was it her dowry bestowed on her as her final home by her son? William of Malmesbury tells of how the Holy Cemetery (at Glastonbury) was the haunt of Kings as well as countless pilgrims, and how many holy men and women sought burial there choosing 'to await the day of resurrection under the protection of the Mother of God' (the medieval title given to Our Lady).

If this was what happened, then all becomes clear and explains the reverence and respect afforded to Glastonbury and its Abbey for 2,000 years. It also explains why succeeding generations of invaders, including the Romans, left Glastonbury untouched whilst sacking the towns and villages which surrounded it.

It was no daydream that inspired William Blake to write his famous hymn, "Jerusalem":

> And did those feet in ancient time
> Walk upon England's mountains green?
> And was the holy lamb of God
> In England's pleasant pastures seen?
> And did the countenance divine
> Shine forth upon our clouded hills?
> And was Jerusalem builded here
> Among those dark satanic mills?
> Bring me my bow of burning gold!
> Bring me my arrows of desire!
> Bring me my spear! O clouds, unfold!
> Bring me my chariot of fire!
> I will not cease from mental fight,
> Nor shall my sword sleep in my hand,
> Till we have built Jerusalem
> In England's green and pleasant land.

His "Dark Satanic Mills" were the Mendip hills: not clear and picturesque as they are today, but shrouded in black clouds of smoke created by the smelting of lead. Blake had been aware of the tradition even as a boy, and was certainly aware of Joseph's arrival with his companions at Wearyall Hill where he is said to have struck his staff, considered by some to have been Christ's own staff, which immediately took root and blossomed. This Glastonbury Thorn, of which there are cuttings in the Abbey and in St John's churchyard, still has a sprig taken from it when it blossoms at Christmastide, as well as at Easter, which is sent to the Queen for display on her Christmas dinner table.

As well as the two cruets containing the blood and sweat of Christ, Joseph is thought to have brought with him the chalice used at the Last Supper and thrown it in the Chalice Well, hence the water's red colour. Today the well is surrounded by beautiful and quite peaceful gardens. However, it is said that at the Dissolution of the Monasteries, a monk took the chalice from Glastonbury – where it had been kept, enhancing the Abbey's

prestige as holding the most Holy of all relics – to Nanteos Manor in Wales. Acting as a priest to the family he bequeathed it to them at his death and they still have it today.

Thought to be the cup used at the Last Supper, it is made not of silver or gold but of olive wood, which certainly makes it sound more authentic than the Holy Grail of precious metal sought by King Arthur and his Knights of the Round Table. About five inches in diameter, it is now much smaller than its original size due to over-zealous cure-seekers nibbling the rim as they drank from the cup. Miracles are still claimed, and although its exact location is not known it is thought to be somewhere in the Cotswolds. Anyone who traces its whereabouts can see and handle it – that being the written rule of the family who hold it.

Joseph is said to have sought out Christ's hut, already hallowed by the presence of Christ, consecrated it, turned it into a chapel, then erected over it, as a form of protection, a much larger wattle and daub church.

This church became the focus of early Christianity in Britain, and when St Augustine came in AD 597 years later to establish a Christian church in Britain he found, to his surprise, Christianity already well established in the South West.

Joseph's church was burnt to the ground during the great fire of 1184 which also

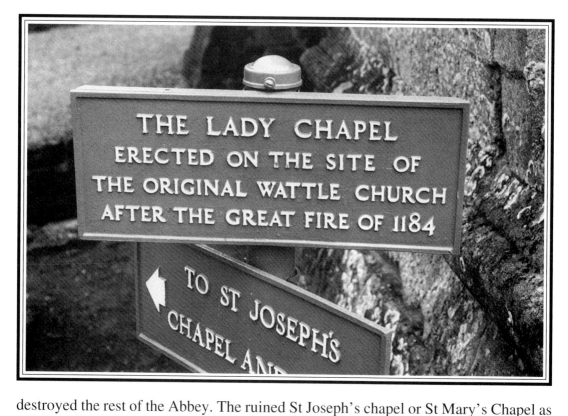

destroyed the rest of the Abbey. The ruined St Joseph's chapel or St Mary's Chapel as it is also known and which we see today was built over the same site. It was here that legend and certain facts have it that Jesus Christ lived on English soil. Is the stone in the external wall of the chapel which states 'JESUS-MARIA' tangible evidence of his mother Mary's presence at Glastonbury?

The Facts

Let us look into the known 'facts', for want of a better word, and trace the legend in more detail.

One theory is that the legend referred to the 'lost land of Lyonesse' located off Land's End. Again let us examine the facts, for it is important to our story. There have been three major earthquakes off the Cornish coast, the last one in about 1090 referred to in the Saxon Chronicle, when everything apart from the tops of the higher ground disappeared under the sea. It is entirely possible that the higher ground is the Isles of Scilly as we know them today.

The map shows the islands at high tide, the hatched area is the land which would be uncovered if the sea level were to sink 65 feet as caused by an earthquake. As recently

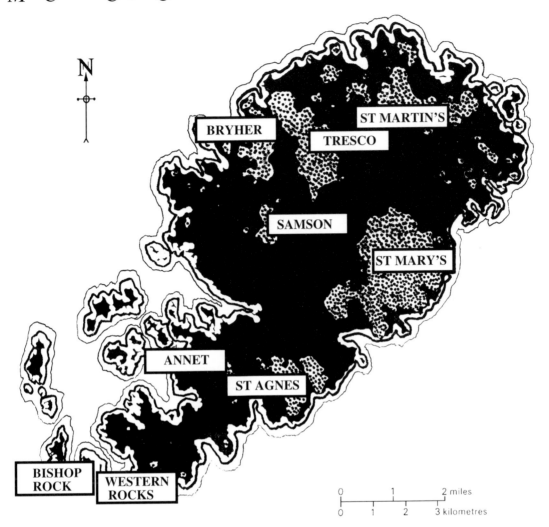

as 1985 a phenomenal low tide linked Samson and Bryher, and folk walked on dry land between them. Was this then Lyonesse or Ictis where Joseph landed to pick up his cargoes of tin and did Jesus walk on Lyonesse?

Certainly other islands on the South coast of Cornwall lay claim to being the legendary Ictus, Looe Island and St Michael's Mount being favourites; although St Michael's Mount comes out on top, being closer to most of the mines, and it has that magical quality which fits so well into our story. Here Celt and Phoenician would have exchanged tales and fables around a fire, as man has done down through the centuries. Probably in clearings within the woodlands which partially surrounded St Michael's Mount at that time. This we certainly know, for at exceptionally low tides traces of that great forest can still be found.

The Celts told their stories but recorded very little. At the time that Christ was alive they were the dominating race, especially in the West Country, and stories of his visits with Joseph of Arimathea would have only been passed down by word of mouth which is how legends, more often than not based on facts, began.

Certainly Jesus' presence was much talked about, and later written about. Support for this part of the tradition is found in historically important documents written by Gildas, the very first British historian, Taliesin, the Druid, St Augustine and the Domesday Book itself. Gildas, writing some time between AD 516 and 570, states: "Christ the True Son afforded his light, the knowledge of his precepts, to this island (Britain) during the height of the last year of the reign of Tiberius Caesar." This suggests quite categorically that Christ's visit as an adult finished before AD 27 when he began his ministry, for Tiberius died in AD 37.

Taliesin, writing in about AD 550, says: "Christ, the Word from the beginning,

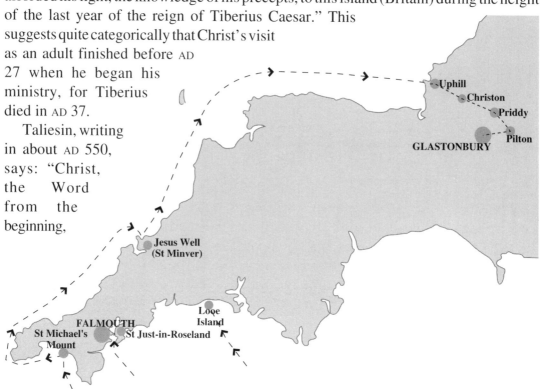

was from the beginning our teacher, and we never lost his teaching."

Now this statement is of particular interest, because at the time of Christ's visit to Britain the Druids had been established for at least 2,000 years, and their basic belief was in a trinity emanating from the godhead Duw. The three golden rays – the emblem of Druidism – were known as Bele the creator of the past, Taran the controller of the present and Yesus (pronounced Jesus!) the coming saviour of the future. Druidism thus anticipated Christianity and pointed to the coming of a saviour – in this country!

Tradition as well as legend has it that Jesus met the Druids whilst an adult at Glastonbury because they were one of the lost tribes of Israel waiting for him here in Britain. Jesus or Yesus, the evidence is certainly there. At that time there were some

60,000 students at 40 Druidic monasteries studying and waiting for his coming, as were the other ancient tribes of Israel, back in the Holy Land.

In a letter to Pope Gregory, St Augustine wrote, "In the Western confines of Britain, there is a certain Royal island (Glastonbury) surrounded by water and on it a church constructed by no human art, but directly constructed by the hands of Christ for the salvation of his people."

From the Domesday Book AD 1086: "The Domus Dei (Home of God) in the great Monastery of Glastonbury called the Secret of the Lord, this Glastonbury church possesses in its own villa XII hides of Land which have never paid tax." These hides of land were given to Joseph and his companions when they arrived after the crucifixion, no doubt as a gift, to support their church built over Christ's original hut. The stone marking the boundary of the further most of the twelve hides can still be found at the edge of Pilton churchyard.

The Journeys

Let us then trace Christ's first arrival to these shores with Joseph of Arimathea. He could have landed at St George's on Looe Island, there are certainly strong claims. There are further claims of landings at Falmouth, fine estuary that it is. Tradition has it that he landed at the Strand, crossed the stream and went up Smithwich Hill.

St Just-in-Roseland is the most popular of his landing places. In St Just Creek there

is a flat stone with strange markings where he first set foot, and he could quite well have done, for St Just-in-Roseland has a Church set in a remarkable Churchyard.

The name has nothing to do with roses, it comes from the old Cornish word 'ruse' meaning promontory, and St Just was one of the early Cornish hermits who probably lived here.

This little creek just off Carrick Roads has probably played its part in the nation's history. From the 1800s there was a quarantine port at Falmouth, just across the estuary.

Ships rested here after Trafalgar and, at the turn of this century, it was very nearly the site of the new naval base. Mercifully Devonport was chosen instead.

I wonder is this the perfect churchyard garden? The simple answer is 'yes', for the churchyard is considered to be the finest in the world: one big beautiful garden. And quite frankly the atmosphere of this sacred place helps make our legend quite believable. There is hardly a level piece of ground in it as it tumbles down towards church and creek. It is full of sub-tropical trees, plants and shrubs which thrive in the gentle climate of this part of Cornwall, and they owe their presence to John Tresidder. He provided them on his return from Australia in 1887. The lych gate is what is known as a corpse gate, because the word lych meant corpse. What happened was that the coffin was brought and laid in the middle where the committal service started. This particular gate is rather different, because if you look carefully you can see how the floor is composed of a series of gridded stones. Known as a Cornish stile it was an early form of cattle grid to keep animals out of the Churchyard.

One of the earliest churches in Britain, St Just dates from Celtic times and is such a peaceful place that people often bring their problems here. There is usually a kindly soul from the village waiting in the Church to offer a sympathetic ear, and I feel certain that visitors must feel the utter peace and comfort which emanates from such a beautiful place with so strong a connection with Jesus Christ and his possible visits to Cornwall.

But for me it has to be St Michael's Mount – still as mysterious a place today as it was all those years ago. From here he must have visited several mines with his uncle, certainly there is talk of him having visited 'Ding Dong' mine in West Cornwall. Further evidence is provided by the fact that Cornish miners sang a song for centuries, the chorus of which runs "Joseph was a miner".

Joseph's business also required that he visit the lead and copper mines at Priddy on the Mendip Hills in Somerset. There is strong traditions of his visit and an age old proverb "As sure as our Lord was at Priddy" is still in use today.

To have reached those lead mines at Priddy, they would have sailed from St Michael's Mount, around Land's End, calling in for water at the 'Jesus Well' at St Minver near Padstow. A well which, over the centuries, has had many miracles attached to it. From there they would have continued up the Bristol Channel, landing at Uphill which is near Weston-super-Mare.

Somerset at that time was very different to the Somerset we know today, for much of it was waterlogged. As can be seen from the map, the coastline was very different.

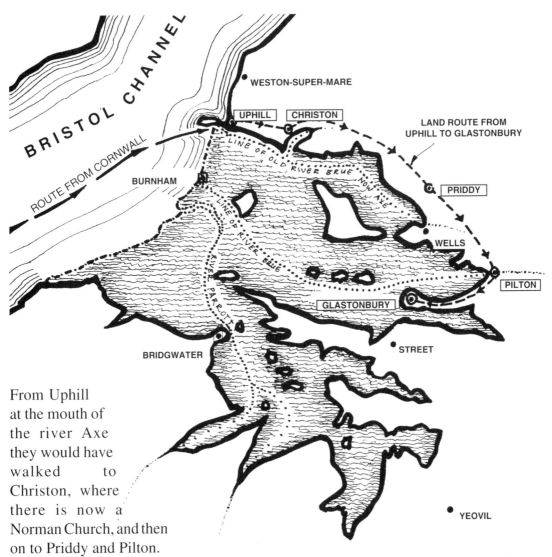

From Uphill at the mouth of the river Axe they would have walked to Christon, where there is now a Norman Church, and then on to Priddy and Pilton.

At Priddy, by way of interesting evidence for consideration, is the church banner which depicts the boy Christ arriving by boat with Joseph. Pilton at that time was a fishing hamlet and it would have been quite easy to sail across to Glastonbury.

In St John's Church, Glastonbury, we find yet another enigma in our story. The great stone tomb in the North transept is considered by some to be the most sacred in the country – Joseph of Arimathea's burial place. This is not generally accepted and is attributed to another worthy personage with the intriguing initials J.A.

The tomb, incidentally, is covered with the cope of Abbot Whiting, the last Abbot of Glastonbury, prior to the Dissolution by Henry VIII.

It was chronicled in 1367 that Joseph lay at Glastonbury, and during the fifteenth and sixteenth centuries it stood in the churchyard where it was revered as a shrine. Many

came on pilgrimages to visit Joseph's tomb. Just another myth – who knows?

Whether fact or fiction, the whole story is beautifully illustrated in the transept's glorious stained glass window overlooking the tomb.

So did Jesus really come here to the South West, as a boy and later as a young man? Is his mother the Virgin Mary buried at Glastonbury? The evidence is there for you to make up your own mind. I admit to being a romantic, and can see him more as a young man spending 'years in the wilderness' on the Island of Glastonbury, rather than in strife torn Palestine preparing for his ministry to the Holy Land, ministering at the same time to the Druids – one of the lost tribes of Israel.

I can see Joseph of Arimathea and his companions arriving at Wearyall Hill, seeking Christ's mud hut and transforming it into a shrine – the cradle of Christianity in this country? Just to be in Glastonbury where he is said to have lived and where his mother may well be buried, is enough for me – how about you?

•••━━◉◗━━•••

⋙ *Four* ⋘
FOLLIES

Royal Crescent
BATH, AVON

Some of our strangest buildings are follies. Not necessarily buildings, but strange structures as contrasting as bridge or temple, grotto or prospect tower. They were usually built by rich eighteenth or nineteenth century landowners with little to occupy their time other than to spend their money indulging their fancies. This they did by erecting ornamental buildings and sham castles on their estates. Admittedly many enhanced the landscape adding romanticism to the English countryside, but sometimes it is difficult to recognise what a folly really is.

Take the quite splendid Royal Crescent at Bath. Hardly a folly, surely, but one of Europe's finest terraces. Well it is certainly the latter, but also, for me, it falls within the fringes of folly definition. For a start, and for all its splendour, it was, when built, a perfect example of spec building. Yes, speculative development on a massive scale.

Many of the famous Georgian architects, particularly those who lived in spa towns or cities like Bath, were also speculative developers and often builders as well.

John Wood the elder, and his son, unimaginatively known by one and all as John Wood the younger, were the top architectural spec building/development team at Bath, and it was the younger Wood who was responsible for the Royal Crescent.

It can certainly boast of many famous residents, factual as well as fictional folk, who, no doubt, returning home late by torch light, would put their torches out on the giant snuffers which still exist.

One famous fellow had his daughter 'pinched', and there is a plaque to prove it. Apparently Richard Brinsley Sheridan eloped with Thomas Linley's daughter. All I can say is that I hope he had a long ladder, particularly if her bedroom was on the top floor!

Another resident who must have appreciated the massive Ionic capitals and columns was Sir Isaac Pitman, inventor of the shorthand system.

Charles Dickens stayed in nearby St James Square. Obviously the Royal Crescent was too posh for him. However it did not stop him lodging his famous fictional character Mr Pickwick there.

What is wrong with spec development anyway? Speaking as an architect, very little when it is on such a grand scale as this. It was certainly a flash of architectural genius that inspired Wood the Younger to take a straight terrace of these glorious houses and bend them into the wonderful crescent shape.

So where and why does the word folly raise its eccentric head? Well, it is not so much an eccentric head as an ugly mug. The backs of that glorious crescent are simply an ugly mess.

What happened was simply this: the Woods put up the façade and sold each section off with a building plot at the rear. The punters, having bought their plot, then put up whatever they liked by way of a dwelling behind the façaded front, which was no more than a screen.

What a folly! What a contrast to that elegant front!

Powderham Belvedere
DEVON

Although it looks like a castle, the Belvedere in the grounds of Powderham Castle is

a viewing tower built on high ground to quite simply take advantage of the view. It also acts as an 'eye catcher' enhancing the landscape.

Built in 1773 of brick and covered in Roman cement, it has been badly vandalised and whilst there are long-term plans for its restoration it, for me at any rate, is a fascinating ruin.

The word belvedere quite simply means 'three-sided tower'.

Haunting rather than haunted, it is rather reminiscent of places featured in heavy Victorian Gothic novels and prose.

Chilton Priory
SOMERSET

The first glimpse of Chilton Priory leaves you confused. This is not a priory or a church, it looks like a house. Therein lies the enigma of the place: though not deliberately built as a folly, it has all the prime characteristics of one, visual confusion being foremost amongst them.

However, analysis proves that it really is a house, built around the original tower dating from 1570, by local man and inveterate collector William Stragling. He acquired the tower in the 1830s, had it restored and increased in height, adding a chapel on the east side. The house itself is largely composed of material salvaged from other buildings, churches, castles, abbeys and even old houses. He was was one of the early conservationists

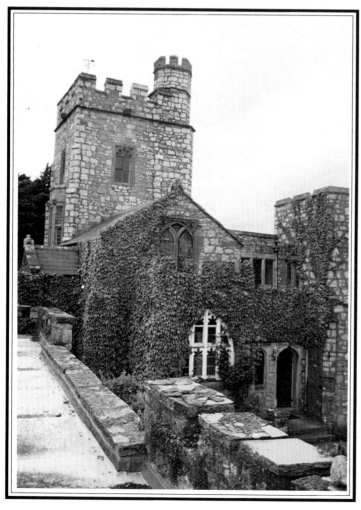

who did not like to think of man-made artifacts being destroyed or discarded. He acquired this mass of stuff and commissioned an architect to design this quite fascinating place.

The battlements and staircase are thought to have come from nearby Chedzoy church, whilst the main mullion window came from a large old country house in the process of demolition, hence the appearance seeming older than it might otherwise have been. It is semi-ecclesiastical in style, and when the building was completed it housed William Stragling's private collection, consisting of items which he had acquired from all over the world. He eventually wrote a book about the house, describing the contents, how he had acquired them, and even adding their current value. It is not surprising that local people were calling it a folly even then.

Its real purpose, however, was to house a private masonic temple, for William Stragling was a prominent Freemason. Even the roof timbers are decorated in masonic colours.

Items were added at a later date when it ceased to be a masonic temple. Sculptress Katherine Maltwood took the house as a summer residence between 1917 and 1938.

She created an amazing piece of sculpture known as Alma Mater, implying that God was a female, an outrageous conception at that time. The figure is banked on either side by an amazing impression of life and death, with human figures clawing their way upwards from the pit of hell towards heaven.

The various coats of arms over the fireplace are presumed to be those of Stragling's children who married into titled families: the Ansteys, Adams and Skinners.

The large coat of arms over the fireplace is Stragling's own.

The room has, in its time, served as both a chapel and a masonic lodge. Alternate black and white flooring, common to masonic lodges, is still here although the fine paintings and tapestries from his collection, which once filled the walls, have long since gone.

The stained glass window is a composite, the glass having been salvaged from cathedrals, abbeys and churches by Stragling.

It was from the top of the tower, overlooking the Somerset levels, that Katherine Maltwood is said to have had the vision which gave rise to her theory of the giant Glastonbury Zodiac. That theory, which I explained in depth in the first *"Cobblestones, Cottages and Castles"* book, was that a massive Zodiac, modelled amongst the hills, ancient trackways and rivers and covering some 10 miles in diameter, was centred around Glastonbury. People today are sceptical of that theory but, at the time, it was hailed as something quite extraordinary by the Bloomsbury set to which she belonged with her husband John.

He was a very wealthy man, who made his fortune by inventing the OXO cube! She refers to the Zodiac as her "Temple of Stars" and relates it to King Arthur's Round Table. Her suggestion is that it is the Round Table of Avalon; a timetable of the sun, moon and planets, whose sky path is the Zodiac. Well who knows?

Certainly she was obsessed by both the Arthurian legend and the legend concerning Joseph of Arimathea and the boy Christ's presence at Glastonbury. So much so that she sculpted a tablet, containing her interpretation of the Arimathean legend. It rests against a garden wall today, but was once free-standing on a nearby lawn. She called the area around that lawn, now unidentifiable, her Isle of Avalon and it was situated in a position which afforded her a clear view of Glastonbury Tor.

No self respecting house, albeit a folly itself, was complete without its grotto, and Chilton Priory is no exception. Dark and grim, it is tucked away below ground, only reachable through a series of high banks and tunnels.

What is intriguing in the grotto is the floor. It is said to be part of an old road which pre-dates the Roman road that once ran along the ridge. If that is the case, then it is yet another aspect of this fascinating house which seems to have such a tantalising history.

Swanage Follies
DORSET

In the 1870s and 1880s John Mowlem and George Burt were changing the face of Swanage, creating something that could well have been the inspiration for Sir Clough Williams-Ellis's Welsh fantasy village Portmeirion – the famous location for the weird cult TV series '*The Prisoner*'. Burt, using his uncle John Mowlem's building firm – still a major contractor today – salvaged bits and pieces from the City of London as it was being demolished and re-installed some of the 'best bits' in the town. Swanage is really enhanced by his so called "follies".

Swanage Town Hall did not use to be a town hall: it started life as the Mercer's Hall in Cheapside, London, in 1670, and was designed by Edward Jerman, one of Sir Christopher Wren's most talented pupils. It came into Mowlem's possession in a most strange way.

Caked with centuries of soot and London grime, examination had proved that it would be cheaper to rebuild than to clean. So it was whipped away to Swanage where, as Mowlem put it, "At this spot nature's cleansers will probably do the work." A breath of sea air has done it the world of good, for it stands today as fresh and pristine as it did when it was first built.

George Burt built himself a glorious property, Purbeck House. Now a convent, it is partially built from pieces, again rescued from London. Inside, he built a private masonic temple, very much the mode of the rich during the later part of the last century. Today it is a chapel.

The external sculpture is a reproduction of part of the Parthenon frieze. With its prancing horses, this was actually bought from one of the great London Exhibitions.

An arched gateway in the garden is intriguing; it was first erected by the Mowlems as contractors at Hyde Park Corner in 1844. When the Corner was improved later in 1883, it was in the way; the main contractors chosen for the work were Mowlems. Burt, by then the major shareholder in the firm, bought it back for a proverbial song and put it up in his garden. So not only did he make a double profit, but he got to keep the edifice as well. A major feature of the arch is the river god Neptune: he recently had his beard trimmed by a flash of lightning!

Someone not quite so lucky was Charles I: lightning has struck twice for him as he has lost his head for a second time. One of two headless statues purchased by Burt for the modest sum of £9, his companion is a headless Charles II. They now stand in front of a "mixed up" Chinese temple, occupying a more modest position than it originally occupied on the Royal Exchange! The temple is not entirely authentic in so far as the columns were taken from a toll house on old Waterloo Bridge!

Burt also built a castle in Swanage. Durlston Castle is now a restaurant, and covering the sides of the building are educational inscriptions, most of them of a geographical or astrological nature.

Below the Castle is the most famous of all Burt's follies, the Great Globe. Massive

– 10 feet in diameter and weighing 40 tons – it is surrounded by plaques, covered in inscriptions describing the world's most famous places. There is even a plain surface provided for rival graffiti artists!

Swanage is packed full of many other fascinating bits and pieces but none more so than Mowlem's greatest folly: the plain granite column on the sea front. He really had his tongue in his cheek here, for it commemorates a non-existent event: the defeat of the Danish fleet by King Alfred in AD 877. To complete the

incongruity of the hoax there are four eighth century cannon balls on top!

Such was his eccentricity that he is even buried in an eccentric tomb in the town's cemetery. You cannot miss it, for it is a tall structure which is neither a spire nor a pyramid, but an incongruous mixture of both. Where else would such a man be buried?

As you walk through the town you can not help thinking what a magnificent rescue job George Burt made, and how grateful the people of Swanage must be today. As we are prone to say, "Shall we ever see his like again?" Sadly, I doubt it. Most of London's contemporary buildings are built of fragile fabrics and unlikely to stand long enough to enjoy a move to the seaside as did the Swanage follies.

Mount Edgcumbe
PLYMOUTH

Mount Edgcumbe, the seat of the Edgcumbe family, overlooks Plymouth Sound and is now a Plymouth park, although administratively still in Cornwall.

The folly is known as the Ruin, and when built was originally in Devon; Cornwall taking over Mount Edgcumbe in 1844.

The sham ruin is thought to have been built much earlier in 1750 by Timothy Brett, and is a superb example of a good sham ruin.

The position overlooking Plymouth city and the Sound is spectacular. Ruination is

extensive, yet the large traceried window offering the view is high enough above the ground to give a differently angled view of the Sound.

Also within the grounds is a beautifully restored shell house, which is really a grotto. Surprisingly, it is situated above, rather than below ground. Such places go back a long way in history, for the Romans built artificial caves in their gardens, no doubt as a sort of decorative sun shelter. They were usually lined with rocks, pumice and shells.

It is not surprising that they became fashionable again in Italy during the Renaissance, or that the English aristocracy, with their love of seashells, adapted them as shelters – more often to keep off the rain than the sun! For, rather like today's back garden swimming pools, they were status symbols.

In a way it seems strange that shells should be used for decorative purposes – they are, after all, geometrically inaccurate – but they were attractive and easily collectable. I am surprised some twentieth century eccentric has not started a similar fashion using old nuts and bolts! Coming in all shapes and sizes as they do, I'm sure they could make equally attractive patterns.

Dulverton Workhouse
SOMERSET

Perhaps man's greatest folly of all is his inhumanity to his fellow beings. Whilst the rich had little else to do but indulge in their fantasies and follies, ordinary folk went in their thousands to the workhouse door seeking a free crust of bread, often exchanging one form of indignity for another. We would be foolish to think that poverty in one form or another does not still exist today, but at least the cruelty which accompanied workhouse life is no longer with us. Inhuman segregation of husband and wife, brother and sister, or the pitifully cruel practice which required an unmarried mother to remain in the workhouse until the child reached the age of thirteen, were very much realities. No freedom, and the stigma of being branded a pauper: what a price to pay for food and a roof over your head. Still, at least the roof of the former Dulverton workhouse covered a fine building.

Its appearance is more in keeping with a small stately home than a workhouse, for good reason. The parish church was being renovated, so the guardians, being more benevolent than most, approached the architect who agreed to design them a new workhouse.

Three standard layout plans were in general use, all were grim in concept, so the architect decided that his workhouse should look more like a country squire's residence, which is why Dulverton could boast of the most attractive looking workhouse in the country. Today this attractive building is Exmoor National Park headquarters.

However, aesthetic appearance could no way compensate for the harsh realities which occurred inside. There were gaunt, cheerless dormitories, and the diet sheets make grim reading: a strict diet, mainly bread and water, with meat only occasionally on a Sunday.

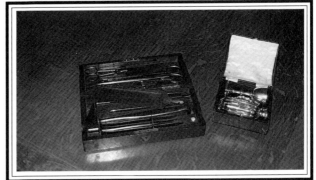

The workhouse surgeon's kit looks like a gruesome tool kit, an all-purpose kit including saws for cutting off limbs and pliers for the drawing of teeth. No anaesthetics either, just a friend or two to hold you down or, if you were really lucky, a swig of the Workhouse Master's cooking sherry! If you survived, then you had the bonus of a bread ticket to obtain a few extra rations to help aid your recovery. These bread tickets had to be taken to the local baker who was very often a miller as well. The ticket entitled the bearer to one loaf, apparently one week's allowance.

If you did not look as if you were going to make it, then the visiting priest arrived, complete with his travelling kit of communion vessels.

The former exercise yard is now an attractive garden, but even when exercising the inmates were separated. The yard originally had a central dividing wall for that purpose. The turret house had a bell which summoned them to meals and sounded their curfew.

I doubt whether many holiday walkers visiting the headquarters today would appreciate the enforced exercise which was compulsory years ago.

Even in death they were segregated, for in the churchyard the inmates were buried in paupers graves situated in the bleak north side of the graveyard. It seems that in 'God's Little Acre' they were still second class human beings; even death was no leveller.

Five
BARS AND JARS

Coach and Horses
BUCKLAND BREWER, DEVON

There is something about a horse-drawn vehicle that is so different from any other form of transport; perhaps it is because we so often view the past through rose-coloured spectacles. Whilst it was not always all that it was cracked up to be, there were certain aspects of life which, for me at any rate, were attractive, and a very comfortable ride in an open landau has to be one of the best.

We were on our way to the appropriately named 'Coach and Horses' pub at Buckland Brewer in North Devon, to look into an unusual, almost macabre, phase of its history.

The hostelry dates from the early part of the thirteenth century, having been put up initially as accommodation for travelling masons and other ecclesiastical craftsmen who were building the parish Church.

Later, it became the village pub, but even then it was not all beer and skittles. The story, apochryphal or otherwise, is that it also doubled up as a courthouse. It is a pleasant place today, but justice was not only done, it was seen to be done, for criminals were tried, sentenced and, if condemned to death, they were hanged through a trap door in the bar ceiling. The rope was said to have been threaded through a hook in the bedroom above. Well, true or false, it is now a delightful hostelry and well worth a visit.

Chagford
DEVON

Y ears ago, the assessing and stamping of tin mined on Dartmoor was the privilege of just four stannary towns. One such town was Chagford. Today it is predominantly a holiday centre, located high up on the north-east edge of the moor. At the centre of the square is the very much restored multi-sided market cross. Originally open, it is now partially filled in with pleasant shops, the remaining area suffering the ignominious fate we often seem to reserve for such historic structures: that of becoming a public convenience.

The parish church stands resplendent in a churchyard surrounded by lovely houses. It was inside this church, built of Dartmoor granite during the fifteenth century, that an incident occurred which was to inspire one of our greatest novelists.

In 1641, Mary Whiddon, who was a member of one of the local ruling families – probably the local ruling family in Chagford, stood at the altar about to take her wedding vows. A shot rang out and she fell mortally wounded to the floor of the chancel. An unsuccessful suitor with the worst intentions in the world had been equally unsuccessful as a marksman: he had tried to shoot her husband to be, missed him and shot her by mistake. She rests where she fell, beneath a commemorative stone. This incident is thought to have inspired West Country novelist R.D. Blackmoor to write '*Lorna Doone*', but for once fiction was stranger than fact: Lorna lived in the book but, sadly, Mary died.

Close by is the tomb of one of her relations, her grandfather, Sir John Whiddon, who died in 1575. It is an early Renaissance tomb. The transition between Gothic architecture and the use of the classic orders which was drifting in from Italy reached this tiny village church very early on. It is a remarkable piece of work for two reasons: one is that it features ten mermaids and mermen on it, and the other is that Sir John's effigy is missing. Normally you would expect to find a reclining figure of the deceased, but nobody knows where it is. It has to be around somewhere.

One place it certainly is not is at his old family home, the manor house which, several hundred years ago, became a hostelry, the Three Crowns Hotel. It is a glorious Tudor house with traditional drip stones over the windows and relieving arches built into the wall above in order to take the pressure off the stone lintels.

They seemed to be a pretty handy lot with their pistols in Chagford in those days, for just a couple of years after Mary Whiddon's death in the church, a young poet, cavalier

Sydney Godolphin was shot during a Civil War skirmish in 1643 and died in the porch on a seat which is still there.

It was at the time of the Civil War that parliament, hard pressed and seeking extra revenue to continue the conflict, slapped a tax on beer. That tax was six pence a barrel, and brewers and landlords alike reckoned that such a tax would be their ruination. Times don't change do they!

At that time the bar itself did not look as it does today. The counter was a simple trestle table, and not at all the focus of attention. It was the fire place which drew the customers, travellers arriving would make for the fire before even seeking a drink. Therein lies the story of the 'pub', because hostelries really started as rest houses put up by the monks

adjacent to their monasteries in order to look after pilgrims and traders. They continued as such until the dissolution of the monasteries by Henry VIII. The only things he spared were the rest houses, which eventually became pubs as we know them today.

The Tom Cobley Tavern
SPREYTON, DEVON

I have to admit to thinking that Uncle Tom Cobley and his friends who rode their grey mare to Widecombe Fair were merely legendary figures. But in the churchyard at Spreyton, a village which claims, incidentally, to be at the exact centre of Devon, I was proved wrong. For this is where the man himself, Thomas Cobley, is buried.

A landowner of some substance, he was born in the Parish in 1762. His companions came from the area and they made their journeys together in the early 1800s. Tom died at the ripe old age of 82, but there's more than his simple gravestone to remind us of his presence, for he started his famous journeys from the village pub.

For me one companion, Oliver, is plenty enough but Tom made his journeys with six companions, all of them remembered in the famous song.

"Tom Pearce,Tom Pearce lend me your grey mare.
All along, down along out along lee
For I want for to go down to Widdicombe Fair
With Bill Brewer, Jan Stewer, Peter Gurney, Peter Davy,
Dannel Whiddon, 'Arry 'Awk,
Old Uncle Tom Cobley and all
Old Uncle Tom Cobley and all."

We may well laugh at songs such as this, but they are records of social behaviour at the time. The thought of half a dozen or so chaps out on a binge, all on one horse,

is quite funny to us. Today just about everyone has his or her own car, but back in the last century, seven men rode on one horse simply because that was all the transport they had, or could afford, between them. It was not just the poor horse but the poor people as well. The pub, with a portrait of old Tom on the sign, was first licensed in 1589 when it was known as 'The White Hart'.

Inside the bar there is a portrait of the grand old man himself. Apparently he and his friends made several journeys to the Fair, but it was the last trip which was commemorated in the famous song. All of them rode on the poor horse to Widecombe, some 18 miles away. There was a sad outcome for, not surprisingly, the load was too much and the old grey mare died.

The George Inn
NORTON ST PHILIP, SOMERSET

The George Inn at Norton St Philip in Somerset claims that it has the longest running licence; unbroken since 1397. It certainly was here dispensing ale in those early days, but as to a licence, well, licenses as such were apparently not issued until 1552, during the reign of Edward VI. But so what. It is a beautiful place and I go along with their claim. It is after all one of the most famous inns in the country.

Why such a large pub in a small village? It was built by Carthusian monks as a wool market, and the great room which runs the whole length of the top storey served as the local market. The upper storeys are half-timbered and stand on a stone-built ground floor. As the centre of Somerset's once thriving medieval wool trade, accommodation was required by both wool merchants and passing traders, so it could be said that the inn developed from the roof downwards.

The inn yard hardly seems to have changed at all over the centuries. The romantic-looking long gallery served a more sinister purpose, for it is said that Judge Jeffreys tried some of Monmouth's supporters from here.

It seems logical that Judge Jeffreys should have held a court here, for Monmouth made it his headquarters prior to the tragic battle of Sedgemoor. That he was here there is no doubt. Apparently he looked out of a window on the first floor, and an assassin, set on gaining the reward offered for his life, fired at the Duke – and missed! It was a costly error, for a copy of a proclamation in the bar states that the reward was five thousand pounds, an immense fortune in those days.

Apart from providing access to the residential part of the inn, the steps adjoining the great entrance door also served as a mounting block for stagecoach passengers.

Unlike most ancient hostelries, security was excellent here as a collection of locks and handles on show in the passage prove. Although we have always been one of the great beer-drinking nations, English ale in those early days had only a short life, for it was not beer as such. It was the Dutch, during the fifteenth century, who introduced hops which, added to the English ale, made beer as we know it today. One man who appreciated locally brewed beer was Samuel Pepys who, with his wife and servants, dined here on June 12th 1668 for just ten shillings.

On the top floor, where the wool market was held, you can clearly see the structure of the

ancient roof. Like the roof timbers, the wooden lintels over the windows have now been here for just over 700 years, for building work started in 1223 and there is hardly a sign of decay anywhere. They certainly knew how to build in those days. Although the floor is constructed of timber, a sort of screed was used to cover it based on a mixture of sawdust and cider.

For me, the George is one of the very few buildings open to the public where you can still sense the dramas which have taken place within its walls.

George and Pilgrims
GLASTONBURY

Glastonbury dominates an area which was for centuries the centre of Christian worship in this country. Whilst the Glastonbury thorn, said to have been Joseph of Arimathea's staff, provides a tangible link with Glastonbury's religious past, another even more tangible link stands proudly in the High Street. It is the George and Pilgrims Inn.

Pilgrims flocked to Glastonbury Abbey and the Abbot, obliged through Christian charity to offer them shelter, built the guest house as accommodation in 1475. It is considered to be the finest example of the period in the country. There is no doubt that its appearance is unusual, for it looks more like part of a church than a pub.

It became an inn, as such, at the dissolution of the monasteries and it is said that Henry VIII watched the burning of the abbey from one of the windows. I find it very interesting that this inn, built all that time ago of local freestone, has stood up to the elements better than its neighbour, a stone built bank.

Built in 1885, it has a splendid pseudo-Gothic front which is a mere 34 feet wide. One has the feeling of entering a much larger building.

The interior has hardly changed at all since the days when succeeding abbots entertained their guests. The abbot's parlour and kitchen, with coffered ceilings and timber walls, are now the bar and a lounge.

Some of the original stained glass remains, further enhancing the feeling of it being an ecclesiastical building.

The abbot's generosity was limited to just two days hospitality. After that you paid your own way. Generations of paint have been removed from the fireplace, taking it back to the original stone.

The room from which Henry VIII probably viewed the destruction of the abbey has a generous fireplace and is still used as a bedroom today, boasting a four poster bed.

Along the passage way is the 'confessional' which is not, as I thought, a polite way of referring to the bathroom and toilet, but merely the doorway to another bedroom.

From the roof you can see the former market place. The ancient market cross was replaced in early Victorian times by a Victorian version of an Eleanor Cross.

The 'George and Pilgrims' has been popular throughout history, and never more than during the great coaching era.

The days when the abbots of Glastonbury flew their flag here have long since gone, but at least you will find the Union Flag still proudly flies over one of England's finest historic coaching inns.

The Turf Hotel
NEAR EXETER

It may well have been Henry VIII that founded the contemporary pub, but it was the Egyptians, some 5,000 years earlier, who actually produced the first glass of ale. They discovered that a micro-organism called yeast turned the sugar content of malted barley into alcohol. They introduced it to the trading Phoenicians who, in turn, brought it to this country. It is not surprising that the wine-drinking Romans, who brought so much that was new to our country, were taken aback to find that the English were already one up on them, at least as far as drink was concerned, for they were brewing something much better – beer.

Having made Exeter a major port, Roman trading vessels were free to sail up the river Exe for several hundreds of years. This continued right up until 1290, when the Countess of Devonshire, in dispute with the city, attempted to throttle Exeter's trade by building weirs across the river. Countess Weir still exists in name today. Whilst not good for Exeter, it helped Topsham develop as a major port. It took until 1564 to sort things out, when the first canal was cut, restoring some trade to the city but never quite allowing it to regain its former importance. Perhaps this is understandable because the engineer, John Trew, only fashioned a waterway which was 1¾ miles long, 16 feet wide and 3 feet

deep – only ten ton tub boats could proceed along it and even they couldn't in certain conditions.

The Exeter Canal, the only ship canal in Devon, that we see today reached its present size and length having been enlarged several times.

The Turf Hotel at its southern end was built about the same time on this promontory between river and canal. "Turf" is actually an ancient name for such a spit of land. It is a fine Georgian building, with the exterior walls hung with tiles. Something quite unusual really, no doubt acting as a sort of 'oilskin' to the main fabric due to its extremely exposed position.

Beautifully sited, there are only two ways to reach it: a gentle twenty minute walk or a delightful canal trip on board the *"Water Mongoose"*.

The important part pubs have played in our way of life is reflected in our literature. From familiar fictional characters like Tom Jones to Charles Dickens' infamous rogue Bill Sykes.

Interestingly enough, it was in an inn yard that the first play was ever performed, and the first music hall presented. If you think about it, today's theatre is no more than a sophisticated development of the inn yard, with its galleries overlooking it.

The pub has contributed so much to the British way of life, and I'm sure that it will continue to be a focal point for us all, now and in the future.

~~ *Six* ~~

GOD'S ACRE

Ottery St Mary Church
DEVON

The parish church of Ottery St Mary is considered by many lovers of church architecture to be the most glorious church in Devon. But it is much more than a church: it is really a mini cathedral, built by some of the same craftsmen who built Exeter Cathedral. The twin towers built over the transepts are direct copies of those at Exeter. It was in 1335 that Bishop de Grandisson of Exeter turned a village church into a village cathedral, something unique in this country. He founded a college of forty monks, and the posts of governors of that college still exist today.

It is the fact that our parish churches often provide a continuous record of a thousand years of history that I must say fascinates me, and it is the little details that often come as such a surprise. Take the elephant's head, carved on a pier close to the back of the Church in 1520. The craftsman who carved it was relying on handed-down information. Never having seen an elephant, his work is quite wonderfully accurate. The only trouble is that, having been told it

had ears, and without a description of them, he gave his elephant human ears! It is such details as this that give us some idea of how people lived and reacted in those days, and of course how they dressed. Take the effigy of Sir Otho de Grandisson. He was the brother of the bishop, and he died in 1539. Resplendent, complete in full armour with his head resting on a helm, he has at his feet a lion, the symbol of strength and vitality. Across the nave, separated in death as they never had been in life, is his wife Lady Beatrix. She is fully dressed, with her hair ornately coiffured, and wearing a long full dress. At her head stand two angels and at her feet rest two dogs which were the sign of fidelity.

If you look carefully, you can see how the faces have actually been removed. This was

carried out by the Puritans because they felt that they were idols and were not the sort of things to be found in Christian places. The Puritans defaced practically every figure in every church at that time. I think what fascinates me most of all at St Mary's is the fact that the chap who originally carved the monument actually worked out what time he was going to have his lunch break from the wonderful clock in the south transept.

It is Bishop Grandisson's clock constructed in the 1340s, and therefore well over 600 years old. Thought to be one of the oldest mechanical clocks in the country, it is still working, and working well. So old is it that it is based on the medieval theory that the earth was the centre of the solar system, with the sun rotating the earth. A 24-hour clock, the hour is indicated by the sun and the phases of the moon by a black and white orb.

The front of the magnificent altar screen was almost destroyed again by the Puritans.

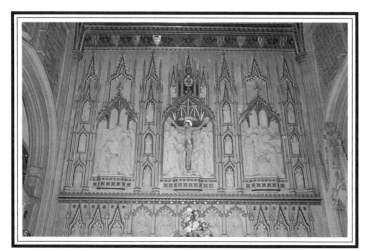

Bits and pieces were chopped off, and some of the figures thrown out. They plastered the remains over, covered it with the ten commandments, and stuck, rather dramatically, the arms of the then monarch right in the middle.

The Victorian restorers took an interest in 1829, and decided that they ought to find out what was underneath. They ripped off the plaster and set about restoring it to its present glory. It was to take another 100 years before restoration was completed in 1935.

High above the chancel is the most magnificent example of vaulting one can find in a parish church anywhere. It was based on the vaulting in Wells Cathedral, where Bishop Grandisson had served for some time. Right in the centre is a lovely boss which shows the holy mother and Christ child, and in 1974 that appropriately formed the centre piece of the eight penny Christmas stamp.

On one wall is the sedilia which is three formal, rather posh seats you might say. They were up-market stalls in which sat the dean, the deacon and the sub-deacon.

The seats normally occupied by the governors are made of wood, and they had to stand for a considerable time during the long services, which often went on for hours and hours. However, they had a trick up their sleeve: when the seat was lifted up, they parked their bottoms on top of the ledge built into the underside of the seat. It was known by the rather splendid name of misericord.

So much of the medieval work has been saved because sensitive Victorian architect William Butterfield was responsible for the restoration work. His own personal contribution was the font, a bit garish even today for some tastes but none the less a fine work of art. This century, thanks are due to the ladies of the congregation who embroidered the superb alter cloth, and to the Friends of the Church of St Mary: through their efforts in 1963 the entire fabric was restored in order to preserve the church for the future generations as a most important part of our great architectural heritage.

Kilkhampton Church
CORNWALL

I suppose one of the most rewarding and cheapest experiences is looking at our old buildings. Admittedly, most of the museums and great country houses charge admittance, as maintenance, in particular, is expensive, but admission to our parish churches is entirely free. Often completely unsupervised, they contain some of our greatest national treasures: not ones of precious metal, but those of wood and stone which are almost a thousand years old. One such treasure house is Kilkhampton Church in North Cornwall,

and tucked inside this porch is perhaps one of its greatest external treasures at any rate, a Norman archway. It is a perfect semi circle. Many experts say that the Norman style of architecture is crude, but that is not so because it was, after all, a copy of the Roman arch. The detail is absolutely superb: there is incut zig zag, some admittedly horrid faces – one chap with his tongue sticking out – but to compensate there are other lovely things, like the delicately carved fir cones.

Incidentally, the porch is the one place in church where you can wear a hat without offence. It is a sort of no-man's-land between church and state. The porch was once put to a variety of uses: they held parish meetings, coroners courts, even school classes, a function which often continued into the nineteenth century.

There were no fixed seats in those early days. Everybody stood. However there was

a range of seats around the perimeter walls, most of them were of stone, and the aged and infirm sat on them. From this has been derived that well known saying, 'Weakest to the wall'. The luxury-loving English did not want to stand and listen to long sermons, they decided to put in pews. They were usually family pews and they remained for generations in the same family. The pews at Kilkhampton are almost perfect examples of rural craftsmanship. If you look very carefully you can see they are made from quite solid hunks of wood, the shelves to take the prayer books are almost as thick as a prayer book. Much of the woodwork has been attacked over the centuries by beetle and worm and is now so worn and hard that it is quite attractive, having taken on the texture and character of granite.

What folk really did was to treat their pews much as they did their homes, upholstering the seats, and in some cases they even put in fireplaces with flues that went up through the columns supporting the roof, although there is no evidence here of such a practice. They actually paid rent for their pews, which had a double advantage. Firstly you could sleep in comfort through the sermon, a common practice for many a sermon lasted at least an hour or more, and secondly you had the right of parliamentary privilege, being allowed to vote for a local M.P. They also tried to get one up on the 'Jones's', because they either had carved their names, or if they had them their coats of arms, on the bench ends to show they were superior to other members of the congregation.

Kilkhampton has 157 different bench ends in all, and they fall into three categories. There are those with coats of arms, there are fascinating religious ones illustrating the Bible stories, but perhaps most curious of all are the ones that contain the mythical beasts.

The jump from sixteenth to eighteenth century craftsmanship is not enormous, but is in complete and colourful contrast. On display are the arms of King George II which were, like many other monuments in the church, designed and executed mostly in plaster by local craftsman Michael Chuke, a pupil of the famous carver Grinling Gibbons. He served his apprenticeship in London, returning soon after to fill the church with some of his finest work. Without doubt his most famous monument is in the Grenville chapel. The memorial is to Sir Bevil Grenville, who was one of Charles I's main Cornish supporters during the Civil war. Sadly he was killed in battle at Bath, and this monument to him is rather grim-looking despite the fine quality of Chuke's work. For whilst it has angels at the corners, it also boasts many weapons of war: guns, pistols, swords, pikes, drums and standards.

Looking around at such treasures, one realises how much they cost to maintain. You never hear of a pub holding a fête to raise money to repair a leaking roof, it is always a church. And I am of the opinion that we should pay when making a visit and put the money raised towards maintenance of the fabric. They do so in France, why shouldn't we do it in this country?

Saint Neot's Parish Church
CORNWALL

Every year at St Neot's Parish Church in Cornwall the branch of an oak tree is fixed to the tower in order to celebrate oak apple day and the fact that Charles II hid in an oak tree prior to his escape from defeat at Worcester.

But St Neot's has something even more fascinating for us: the finest collection of ancient stained glass windows anywhere. If, like me, you thought that church windows were put in just to lighten the place up, I'm afraid we are both mistaken. Back in the middle ages few people could read so the priests used stained glass windows to illustrate the Bible stories. The lovely coloured windows were a sort of strip cartoon, making it easy for everyone to understand the Bible.

One of the most delightful depicts Noah and the flood. We find him on the dockside taking on supplies aboard a ship. Not the traditional "Ark" as we know it but a medieval ship, for they often illustrated their Bible stories with contemporary items and features. It is the equivalent to us showing a cruise liner in a modern window.

Various incidents are well illustrated although it looks a bit crowded, and one or two of the animals have a strange look about them. There is a pigeon or two with a duck and a swan, as

well as the dove Noah sent out looking for the dry land as the waters receded, a charming lion has human ears, and there is at least one unicorn in the background.

Our last glimpse of Noah sadly shows him as the inveterate drunkard he became. I thought they were taking too many barrels on board earlier on!

The original intention of the vicar Parson Tubbe, back in 1508, was to provide a complete history of the Old Testament. He managed to pay for some of the windows himself, but due to lack of funds he was obliged to abandon the project. They were apparently hit by inflation even in those days.

Saddened that he was unable to complete the concept, he did the best thing he could have possibly done – got down on his knees and prayed. The answer was simple, why not get the local wealthy families to pay for them? This they were quite happy to do, as long as they too were included in the window. Although this meant that Parson Tubbe was obliged to abandon his Old Testament theme, he got his windows. And the families successfully perpetuated their image for all time. In one case we can see dad, mum, four sons and eight daughters.

How has all this wonderful glass survived? Well, St Neot's was lucky: the windows were completed just before the Reformation laid its mark of bleak austerity on so many of our parish churches. What is more the church, being off the beaten track, did not draw the attention of Cromwell's Roundheads who had a habit of breaking church windows as a pastime.

It really is beautiful work when you consider how limited the stained glass craftsmen were by their materials.

The Creation, St Neot's oldest and most famous window, has God creating Adam, and could well be eight hundred years old, according to some authorities.

What a remarkably sensitive face God has for such an early illustration. The serpent, with a human face, is tempting Adam and Eve with the apple, and we see Adam taking his bite and Eve taking hers. God, having spotted what they have been up to, chases them from the Garden of Eden, sword in hand, and we find them in the next window, suitably

dressed and working for a living. No Garden of Eden any more for them – just plenty of hard work. We see Adam grafting in the garden with a primitive spade. I never did think apples did you any good, whatever they say!

Meanwhile in another window, left to their own devices, sons Cain and Abel are up to no good. Well, Cain is anyway: he's bumping his brother off. Pardon the colloquialism, but it is a strip cartoon after all, albeit a medieval one.

God spots what has been going on, and this time he really is upset and gives Adam a right telling off. It has all been too much for Adam, and he takes to his bed. Obviously he had need for the

commode at the side of the bed! Another example of a contemporary artifact woven into this finest of all the Bible stories.

What a glorious group of treasures, all paid for by families keen to preserve their image. If you wish to preserve yours, rather than in the family album, why not dedicate a window in your own church? After all, it may well be tax deductible!

Sherborne Abbey
DORSET

I have always been fascinated as to how towns originally got their names. Sherborne comes from the Saxon 'scirebourne', meaning clear stream, and that seems to sum up Sherborne. It is a town which is clean and fresh, and has among its many treasured buildings the Abbey. Tranquillity is the keynote.

It is rare to find an ecclesiastical building which, in its time, has been used as cathedral, monastic church and parish church. It is a parish church today in which are buried two English Saxon kings – Ethelred and Ethelbert, elder brothers of King Alfred the Great.

Of the original cathedral built in 706, little of the Saxon work remains, only slight traces at the west end. Three hundred and seventy years and 27 bishops later, the bishopric moved to Salisbury, and the cathedral became an abbey church. Most of the remaining Norman work is inside, but you can still see beautiful late Norman work in the porch.

It was in the fifteenth century that the older building was transformed to the glorious place that is here for us to visit today. Many of the old monastic buildings remain, but they now form part of Sherborne School. You

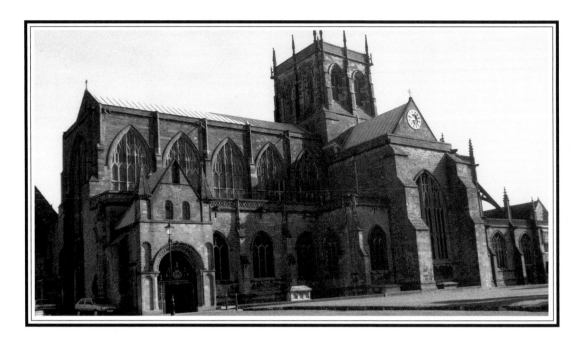

can also see the 'conduit' as it is called locally. It was the monks' washing place. A bit too public to be used today, I am afraid, standing revealed as it does for all to see at the bottom of Cheap Street.

Originally, the parish church of All Hallows had been built against the west end, and you can still see the remains of one of the columns built into the wall. This was demolished, and in keeping with medieval custom, the nave of the abbey was then used as the parish church.

Sherborne Abbey's greatest treasure is the fan vaulting which forms the roof to the nave and choir, and is considered to be the most perfect example in the whole of the country. The great west window is a perfect example of perpendicular architecture, with strong vertical and horizontal feeling. Seen from inside, it is a blaze of colour depicting a variety of Bible stories.

It was the wish of Sir Walter Raleigh, who built and lived in nearby Sherborne Castle, to be buried here. I am sorry that this is not so, for the grave of the founder of the British Empire, together with those of the Saxon kings, would have completely set the seal upon Sherborne Abbey's claim to a major place in English History.

∽Seven ∽
MANOR HOUSES

Lewtrenchard Manor
Devon

*"O*nward, Christian soldiers,
Marching as to war,
With the Cross of Jesus
Going on before.
Christ the Royal Master
Leads against the foe:
Forward into battle,
See, his banners go!
Onward, Christian soldiers,
Marching as to war,
With the Cross of Jesus
Going on before."

The words of that powerful hymn have probably been heard more often in the tiny Devon church at Lewtrenchard than at any other parish church in the country, for the very good reason that they were written here in the last century by the rector the Rev Sabine Baring-Gould. A man of many talents, he stood head and shoulders above his Victorian contemporaries.

Considered to be one of the top writers of his day, he completed 142 books on subjects ranging from West Country songs and folklore to 21 volumes on the 'Lives of the Saints'.

Unlike most Victorians, bent on restoring their churches and homes, he was one of the very few who preserved rather than destroyed the medieval woodwork and other ecclesiastical embellishments which filled them. The original rood screen, riddled with worm and beetle, was thrown out by his grandfather as potential firewood. But young Sabine, fascinated as he was by wonderful old woodwork, took it away and hid it.

He came back 40 years later as rector, and the first thing he did was to locate those sections of woodwork. Sadly they were all damaged and unusable, and he did the only possible thing: he had a new one made. It certainly is a wonderful screen. It was designed and built by the Misses Pinwill of Ermington (see chapter one, pages 20/22). The Pinwill sisters also carved the superb pulpit which was based on the medieval pulpit. It really is absolutely charming, and a fine example of their craftsmanship.

I suppose the '*pièce de résistance*' is the wonderful eagle lectern which he brought back from a tour of Brittany, it having been thrown out there outside of a church. Being the harbourer he was, he brought it back and placed this fine piece of medieval work in the church.

During Saxon times, the line of the village street followed the road and drive to the manor house. Apart from the church, all that remains is the manor house; the rest of the tiny timber dwellings had probably disappeared even before the forceful arrival of William the Conqueror.

The Manor House has changed a great deal since those days. Sabine had inherited it in a sadly dilapidated state, and immediately set about restoring and renovating it. He added a further wing which contains the ballroom, and made the front balance, forming the traditional E-shape plan of the Elizabethan manor house.

Lewtrenchard Manor is now a fine hotel. The entrance lounge is a delightful room with a portrait of Sabine himself painted in his thirties. It was at that time he met and fell

in love with a rather lovely mill girl. She was just sixteen years old, however. Things being as they were in those days, she was not cultured in the social graces, so she was sent away for a year to be brought up to scratch! It is rather interesting, because one of Sabine's great friends was George Bernard Shaw, and he is supposed to have based '*Pygmalion*', later '*My Fair Lady*', upon the early life of Sabine and his delightful mill girl wife.

The ballroom is absolutely magnificent with carving as rich as any decoration to be found on the most elaborate wedding cake, and most of it is Austrian carving which Sabine brought back from Austria. He was at it again rescuing woodwork, this time sixteenth century carving. Odds and ends were missing. What he did was to get hold of one of his estate craftsmen, who incidentally was aged about 60 and sick in bed, and said, "Look, you've got a life's work here, so come on, get up and do this for me!" He did just that. It may be rather ornate for some tastes, but it is a 'bit of Baroque' at the back of beyond.

Sabine Baring Gould financed the estate through his books, and it is said that, with 15 children to feed, his greatest inspiration was hunger. He wrote standing up at a desk during the night between the hours of 10 p.m. and 3 a.m., and the desk now stands underneath his portrait in the entrance lounge. In the morning he rose early, often to tramp his beloved Dartmoor seeking further inspiration.

He died in 1924, aged 89, having helped fill the bookshelves of the British Museum library, and the English Hymnal with at least a dozen hymns and carols and, most of all, having enriched the Devon landscape with his restoration of Lewtrenchard.

Dawnay House
DORSET

Dawnay House at Puddletown in Dorset, though Georgian in date, is built in the Queen Anne style of architecture. A perfect example, illustrating how modern ideas – fashions as well as styles – took their time to filter from the metropolis to the country. Dawnay, however, is not just another country house open to the public; it does its best to create a period atmosphere by use of figures of characters who owned and lived out their lives here over the centuries. The key figure, the Reverend Henry Dawnay, was the fourth son of Viscount Dawnay and, as so often happened years ago, the eldest son went into the army and the youngest into the church.

However they are not all stuffed dummies here, far from it. 'Live' residents, dressed in the appropriate costumes of the period, carry out domestic chores, bringing the whole place to life. You really do feel that you are peeping into the past.

Rooms decorated in the Chinese style were popular during the eighteenth century, and the bed, also in Provincial Chinese Chippendale, is a fine piece of furniture.

Dawnay succeeds so well because each room reflects a different style of life, with appropriate items of the period. In the Victorian salon, the vicar's wife plays the dulcitone to her visitor. An unusual instrument which uses tuning forks and felt tipped hammers to create the sound, a fascinating cross between a musical box and a celeste.

They really have made a fine effort with some of the figures here. The costumes are authentic and some of the models actually look most realistic. In the Dawnay room we find the Reverend Henry Dawnay discussing plans for an extension with his architect. These plans are on the table for us to look at with him.

Entertainment had its limitations in Georgian times. Flirting, dallying and a bit of reading were very nearly it. The rich, however, held *fête champêtres*; grand parties held in the gardens where guests were expected to saunter by the lake side and admire the

statues. Usually one of the greatest attractions were actors, covered in silver or bronze paint, who posed as living statues, moving very occasionally and then only to sprint into a new position to take up a different pose. The usual finale to such events was when one of the figures overlooking a pool, who had not moved at all, would suddenly urinate into it. A fitting climax to such a bawdy event!

Hareston Manor
PLYMOUTH

This fifteenth century manor house in the South Hams is miraculously well preserved. It was far enough off the beaten track to have been forgotten, withstanding the passage of time and what we laughingly refer to today as progress.

Manor means "the whole estate of the lord", not just the building, and was an entirely independent economic unit. All such medieval manor houses were no more than a collection of smaller rooms, grouped around a central hall and courtyard. They started as a series of separate structures, rather like the encampment of a tribal chieftain; but for convenience, security and ultimate visual effect, merged into a tight defensive group around the Great Hall.

In more recent years the manor suffered from neglect, but was lovingly and skillfully restored by the late Ken Bassett to its former splendour and present appearance.

It all happened in the the Great Hall, where life revolved around the great central space, but I am afraid it did not look like it does today with its nice clean walls. The walls would have been covered with smoke, and the whole floor would have been absolutely filthy. It was covered in rushes, obviously to try and achieve some sort of semblance of cleanliness. The dais where the lord and lady and family sat, in order to eat away from the rabble, was at one end. Food dropped on to the floor of the hall was never cleared up, all they did was to scatter reeds and straw on top of the debris. It became known as the marsh area for pretty obvious reasons.

In the centre of the hall was the fireplace. It is hardly right to call it a fireplace, for it was no more than an open area with a fire, the smoke finding its way eventually up through a hole in the roof. Later on, of course they moved the 'fire' place to the side, turning it into a conventional fireplace.

They ate their food quite early in the day, because they were obliged to use natural light. Up at dawn, they would work until dinner time somewhere between 10 and 11 o'clock in the morning, with supper at 4 o'clock. They ate off pattens, great hunks of bread which were used as plates, these they threw onto the floor, when finished, for the dogs, which helped the 'swamp' develop again.

The food came in through the screen to the screen's passage, above which would have been the minstrels' gallery. As soon as they saw the food arriving, they struck up the 'band' and 'played' it to the table. The screen's purpose was to stop the draughts from the front door.

The screen, found in a poor state of repair, has been restored, the dark sections being all that remained of the original screen. Across the screen's passage is the pantry, and next to it is the buttery, presided over by the yeomen of the buttery. In it were stored beer and candles, whilst the bread was kept separately in the pantry.

Hall life was overwhelming, so the lords of the manor decided that they should have a degree of privacy for themselves and their families. An upstairs room was built at the dais end of the hall, called the solar – a French word meaning 'upstairs room'. A feature at Hareston is the tiny chamber off the solar from which the lady of the manor could keep her eye on the often rowdy goings on in the Great Hall below, through a peephole.

The large bedroom was formerly the Great Chamber, a private room for the family which superseded the solar.

The manor was originally planned four square around a central courtyard, the great barn on the east side was a later addition built in 1632.

The chapel, an important and integral part of the estate, is at the north-east end of the home. Built by the lord of the manor as a convenience to both himself and his retainers, it is a mere 12 feet wide by 15 feet long. It was licensed in 1379 by the Bishop of Exeter and dedicated to St Martin who, among others, was also the patron saint of penitent drunkards. It has all the required features of a small church: an altar, a piscina where they washed the vessels, a statuette of the Virgin Mary and a statue of Christ. There is also a holy water stoop. The chapel was re-dedicated in 1978 and used for the christening of the Bassett's first grandchild.

There has been a dwelling on the site of the present manor house for over a thousand years, and with the care and attention which has been given to it by the Bassett family, I am sure that this one will still be here in another thousand years time.

Brympton d'Evercy
NEAR YEOVIL, SOMERSET

There can be few groups of buildings in Britain, let alone the South West, which combine architecture, sentiment, historical association and superb scenery. Brympton d'Evercy near Yeovil in Somerset has all this. It is a magic place which seems to cast a spell over inhabitant and visitor alike. During the last 750 years the estate has been owned by but three families.

The d'Evercy family were first on the scene, but it was the second family, the Sydenhams, who built the fine Tudor west front during the reign of King Henry VIII. They had strong ties with the Blood Royal, and were allowed to display the Royal Arms on their property.

The porch is of later date than the front, but being built of golden Hamstone it blends in well.

The third family to own the estate were the Fane family, and Charles Clive-Ponsonby-Fane was determined to preserve the house – something he has achieved with Judy, his wife.

Together with friends and helpers she made an enormous tapestry called the "Great Rug": 23 feet long, 9 feet high and hand woven like a rug. Based on a drawing of the house, it weighs 200 lbs, has a third of a million knots in it and took 2,500 hours to make.

Constructed entirely of timber, the stairway is the longest straight flight in the country. Fixed against an external wall, it has no less than four intermediate landings.

There are many stories about the family, but the one which, to me, is the most fascinating concerns Lady Georgiana Fane. She never married, having lost her heart to a young ADC of her father, who was at the time Viceroy of Ireland. When the young subaltern asked for Lady Fane's hand in marriage, he was firmly put in his place. He was told that such a 'lowly soldier' was a quite unsuitable match for an Earl's daughter. That 'lowly soldier' went on to become better known as the Duke of Wellington.

It was Lady Georgiana Fane who was responsible for the lake. Actually it is known by the family as the pond – some pond!

She was also responsible for the formal layout of the gardens, planting thousands of oak trees around the estate.

Despite not having got her way about marrying the future Duke of Wellington, she must have been some 'tough cookie', for entirely on her own she negotiated directly with Brunel for the sale of estate land on which was subsequently built the Yeovil to Taunton railway line.

The house had come into the Fane family's ownership in 1731 when Francis Fane,

a barrister and M.P., purchased it at auction for £15,492 10s, a quite enormous sum at that time. It was during this period that many of the things of beauty and good taste owned by the family originates. For me though, its greatest possession is an architectural enigma: the south front completed some 50 years earlier.

This splendid façade was the work of the equally splendidly named Sir John Posthumous Sydenham. It was once thought to have been designed by Inigo Jones, however it is impossible that he supervised the work, for building started in 1678 – 26 years after his death. Aesthetically it is a disaster. Would the master have made such fundamental mistakes as starting at one end of the house with a pointed lintel over a window and ending the row with a rounded one or, much worse, having as the grand centre piece of this superb façade, a drain pipe? I doubt it very much!

For a ten-year period during the late 1950s and early 1960s Brympton became a school. Living at Brympton had become too expensive for the family, and they moved to the rectory nearby. In 1967 Charles Clive-Ponsonby-Fane repossessed the house from the school, moved back into the family home and set about restoring it, with Judy's help, to its former glory.

Among the fascinating discoveries made at the time was another quite tangible tie with royalty. Scratched into the lead covering of the turret roof are the outline of the footmarks showing where George IV had stood on his visit to Brympton in 1820.

Just over the wall in the churchyard are the family graves. Here they lie tucked up beneath their leafy duvets, patiently awaiting resurrection day. What a lovely idea, for it fills this charming spot with joy, rather than sadness.

The family church is also the parish church. Site of a religious building for 700 years, it is dedicated to St Andrew. Inside this tiny chapel, in the north transept, are the tombs of members of the family going back as far as the fourteenth century.

Outstanding among these is the reclining figure of a commoner. The noble face on this effigy is in loving memory of the parish priest, who unceasingly ministered to the sick and dying during the Black Death of 1348. It was carved by an unknown local mason who was also responsible for the rare nativity scenes in the canopy covering the tomb.

The priest, also unknown by name, continued to care for the sick until eventually, like every one else in the parish, he too died.

The remains of the old preaching cross are the oldest part of Brympton, for the cross was in use long before the church was built. St Andrew's most unusual feature is the oversized bellcote. No doubt the bells were covered in this way to save building a bell tower.

The state rooms have been restored to their former splendour and decorated in their original glorious colours. What a feast, and all the work carried out with love and infinite care by Charles and Judy. There surely can not be a better example of a property held in trust both for his family and for the nation.

———————————— ···◄●◉●►··· ————————————